THE
WEST SOMERSET
RAILWAY

· A PAST and PRESENT COMPANION ·

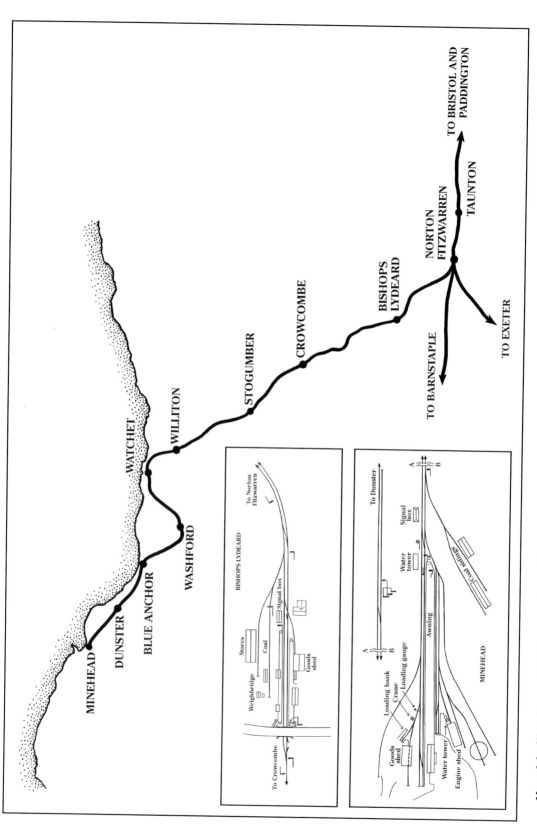

Map of the West Somerset Railway, together with sketch plans of Bishops Lydeard and Minehead stations drawn on the spot in the 1950s by Joe Moss.

THE
WEST SOMERSET
RAILWAY

· A PAST and PRESENT COMPANION ·

A nostalgic trip along the whole route from Taunton to Minehead

John Stretton

· RAILWAY HERITAGE ·
from
The NOSTALGIA Collection

First published in 2000
Reprinted 2008

British Library Cataloguing in Publication Data

A catalogue record for this book is available from the British Library.

ISBN 978 1 85895 166 9

Past & Present Publishing Ltd
The Trundle
Ringstead Road
Great Addington
Kettering
Northants NN14 4BW

Tel/Fax: 01536 330588
email: sales@nostalgiacollection.com
Website: www.nostalgiacollection.com

Map drawn by Christina Siviter

Printed and bound in the Czech Republic

Past and Present

A Past & Present book
from
The NOSTALGIA *Collection*

ACKNOWLEDGEMENTS

As with any project such as this, I am indebted to many organisations and individuals. With this particular book there has not been one that has stood out, but I would be very remiss if I did not thank the following for their ready help with advice, photographs, access, general guidance or proof reading: West Somerset Railway management, Richard Jones, Ian Coleby, Mike Esau, John Gilks, Tom Heavyside, Lens of Sutton, National Monuments Record Office at Swindon, Maurice Dart, Brian Morrison, Western Daily Press, Robin Butterell, Hugh Ballantyne, James Besley, Norman Browne, Richard Casserley, Norman Kneale, Sydney Leleux, Colin Marsden, Millbrook House Ltd, Joe Moss, Allan Stanistreet, Ronald Toop, Peter Treloar, Peter Triggs, and Branston Railway Museum.

There have also been others and their assistance is hereby formally acknowledged. Without them all the book would not have been possible.

Finally I must thank the publishers for their encouragement and patience, and my wife Judi for her constant forbearance at domestic duties often taking second place!

CONTENTS

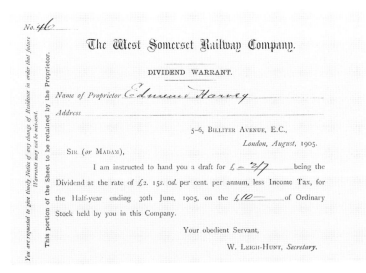

Taunton, the start of our journey, is 163 miles from Paddington and the exchange point for countless thousands of holidaymakers over the years making their way to Minehead by rail. In an undated view, but probably from between the wars and certainly before 1932, when the station through lines were quadrupled, creating an island platform, a down express pauses opposite a delightful GWR period piece, the impressive station signboard. So as not to be left in any doubt, travellers are advised that this is the junction for 'Chard, Minehead and Barnstaple branches'. It could also have included Yeovil. The vista has an extremely busy feel, with a mixed freight in the up bay to the left, a mixed passenger and parcels rake to the right and a throng of people by the express. Note the ample protection from the elements for the travellers, with the attractive overall roof spanning the three tracks seen here. *Crown Copyright, National Monuments Record*

INTRODUCTION

L et me state at the outset that the preparation of this book has been a delight. The other volumes that I have produced in the 'Past & Present' series have all been, in their own ways, joys to compile, and this one has been no exception. Not only is the line an attractive route, but the railway operating it gives the lead to many another in its provisions for and handling of the visiting public. In my various visits to this part of Somerset, I have unfailingly found the staff to be welcoming, cheerful, co-operative, patient and willing to 'go that extra mile' to satisfy my needs. Individually they are probably not aware of the good impression their kindness leaves, but the successful generation of increasing visitor numbers to an area to some extent 'stuck out on a limb', is testament to the appreciation felt by all on the receiving end.

The current West Somerset Railway is the longest line among preserved railways in the UK and, coupled with the scale and quality of restoration over the past quarter of a century, it fully deserves to be classed among the 'Premier' heritage railways. In present-day terms, from a standing start at either end trains climb and twist and turn over 21 miles of testing terrain between Bishops Lydeard and Minehead, with locos and crews having to work hard. This gives the visiting public a 'jolly good show' as a result.

Somewhat like the proverbial football match, the formation of the branch from Norton Fitzwarren to Minehead is virtually a story of two halves! The first section – geographically two-thirds of the final distance – was built by the West Somerset Railway Co, but opened and operated by the Bristol & Exeter Railway as far as Watchet on 31 March 1862, as a 14-mile spur from its main line between the two named cities. This is the reason why Watchet's station buildings are at 90 degrees to the line. The second stretch came a decade later, under the auspices of the Minehead Railway Co, opened to Minehead on 16 July 1874 and again operated by the B&ER. Both were laid out to Brunel's 7ft 0¼in (broad) gauge. However, the junction station at Norton Fitzwarren was not opened until 1873, following the opening of the Barnstaple branch, which diverted from the main line at this point. Conversion to 'standard' (but then considered 'narrow') gauge came in October 1882, and the branch then settled into peaceful normality until the mid-1930s, when the GWR added two passing loops and, over a period of two years, doubled the sections from Minehead to Blue Anchor and Norton Fitzwarren to Bishops Lydeard.

For the last 50 years of normal operation the branch saw a gradual increase in train journeys, excepting the war years, with BR services numbering around ten each way on weekdays (Monday-Saturday) and half a dozen on Sundays. During the summer months there were also through trains to and from Paddington and the Midlands. This traffic was not reflected in the line's financial prosperity, however, and, together with many other branches throughout the country, the influence of increasing affluence among the travelling public and a shift to road transport in the 1950s brought growing losses. In an attempt to staunch the haemorrhage, diesel multiple units (DMUs) were introduced from 10 September 1962. This did little to solve the problem, however, and despite long and vociferous opposition, the line closed on 4 January 1971.

Thankfully, that was not the end of the matter. With a proposal for re-opening the branch, a new West Somerset Railway Co was incorporated on 5 May 1971. A Light Railway Order was obtained in November 1973, and in 1975 a lease was secured from Somerset County Council, who by that time owned the trackbed and surrounding railway land. Necessary preparative and remedial work being completed by the new railway, trains again ran on the branch from

28 March 1976, albeit only from Minehead to Blue Anchor. This short stretch was extended to Williton on 28 August 1976, followed by further progress to Stogumber on 7 May 1978, finally reaching Bishops Lydeard on 9 June 1979. Hopes were for a return to Taunton, but early anticipation was thwarted by British Rail, and later Railtrack, placing obstacles in the way. This goal has not been abandoned, however, and as the new millennium dawns there is perhaps more genuine hope of achieving this Holy Grail: through trains run as specials to Minehead, the privatised freight company EWS has used the branch for access to the coast, one or two Train Operating Companies have murmured regarding restoring rostered through trains, and, perhaps most importantly, there seems to be a slightly more sensible approach from Railtrack over costings for access. The connection to the main line remains at Norton Fitzwarren, with tantalising prospects 'so near and yet so far'!

Public services in the 1990s are well known to visitors to the route and have been well publicised in the railway and local press. The use of the branch to transport stone to Minehead and Doniford for sea and cliff defences has also been well publicised, but what is perhaps less well known has been the use of the line for driver training (by German drivers!) on Class 59s (see page 46) and for training and demonstrations by infrastructure companies. These latter have made good use of the track between Bishops Lydeard and Norton Fitzwarren, where they can operate in safety, without having to break their demonstrations for service trains. Not only does this bring welcome finance to the railway, but it also helps to keep the track in good shape.

So, as the 21st century opens, the West Somerset Railway is perhaps in better health than at any time in its history. With Butlin's holiday camp still very active, leisure activity very much an increasing trend and road traffic congestion leading to many reappraisals of rail routes and travel, the prospects for the West Somerset Railway are extremely encouraging.

This is not the first book on the route, but the 'past and present' comparisons give a different slant and I hope that the reader may derive some of the pleasure that I have enjoyed.

M. John Stretton

Taunton

In a picture full of action and anticipation ex-GWR 'County' Class 4-6-0 No 1019 *County of Merioneth* restarts an unidentified Class B down stopper, probably bound for Exeter, on 31 May 1962. Behind the train in platform 1 a three-car DMU waits its turn for the road, while to the right 2-6-0 No 7326 stands in the bay with a subsequent departure for Barnstaple. Minehead trains also left from this bay on occasions, although mostly they took the tracks on the far side of No 7326. 'Counties' were not normally assigned to Class A duties, but were more than adequate for intermediate express and longer local trains. At this time allocated to 83C Exeter shed, No 1019 later moved to Shrewsbury depot, from where it was withdrawn the following March. *Tom Heavyside*

G. W. R.

TAUNTON

Coming forward 17 years from the previous photograph things have changed dramatically. By 1979 not only has steam disappeared from the scene, but branch lines have also closed and the central platforms at Taunton, Nos 5 and 6, have, since March 1967, lost their passenger facilities. Platform buildings and canopies have been dismantled, leaving just a few trees to enliven an otherwise barren surface. On 16 May 1979 Class 46 No 46009 hauls a rake of china clay empties southwards, bound for Cornwall. New in December 1961 as D146, No 46009 achieved notoriety in July 1984 when it was used in a staged demonstration test collision with a CEGB nuclear flask at Old Dalby, travelling at virtually 100mph. Severely damaged, needless to say it did not work again, being cut up on site over the next three months.

Thankfully no further station demolition has taken place over the last 20 years, and apart from more modern motive power now on show, the only noticeable changes are in the growth of the trees, the more modest station nameboard on the old platform 7, and the removal of the semaphore signal gantries at the far end, which took place around 1985. A First Great Western HST set revs up to leave this platform – now No 2 – with a train bound for Paddington, while at platform 1 passengers are leaving and joining a Class 158 DMU on a South Wales-Penzance service. *Tom Heavyside/MJS*

Platform 3, the 'Barnstaple' bay, is seen again, this time with 'Mogul' No 6337 receiving lubrication attention before a late afternoon departure in the early summer of 1961. To its right, 2-6-2T 'Prairie' tank No 4157 waits to head a train to Minehead from bay platform 4. There is a relaxed air about the scene with, in addition to the casual maintenance from the fireman, a father cradling his child by the Minehead train and a potential traveller squatting on a bench between the two rakes of coaches. Both locomotives were allocated to Taunton at this time, witnessed by their 83B shedplates, but with the closure of branches and reduction in work, both were transferred away; No 6337 ended up at Didcot, from where it was withdrawn in July 1964, while No 4157 travelled north-west, finishing work at Severn Tunnel Junction in June 1965.

Nearly 40 years later, again the scene is much changed. The engine shed closed in October 1964 and, following the closure of the Minehead and Barnstaple branches, the far bay platform became unused. Unattended to, both platform and shed yard have become a burgeoning wildlife garden. While it is perhaps understandable that the few remaining staff have no instructions – or interest? – in attending to the situation, it is not exactly a desirable advertisement for our railways. Apart from the platform canopy on the left, the old repair shop is the only remaining common feature, beside which in August 1999 can be glimpsed one of Railtrack's prestigious Stoneblowers, partly hidden by the undergrowth. *David Johnson, Millbrook House collection/MJS*

Although seen towards the end of steam in the area, Taunton shed yard, buildings and, indeed, the locomotive itself, all wear an appearance that had hardly changed over many decades. In the shed yard in July 1964, just three months before closure, and proudly wearing its home 83B plate, 2-6-0 No 7337 prepares to move off shed to pick up a waiting mineral train in nearby sidings. The engine finished its days at Swindon just three months later. *Jon Marsh*

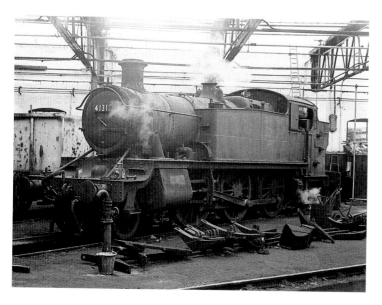

Simmering inside the now roofless part of the shed in July 1964, 2-6-2T No 4131 has just returned from duty on a local pick-up freight. Again leaving the confines of Taunton shortly after this view, No 4131 was withdrawn from Bristol (Barrow Road) shed at the same time as No 7337 above. *Jon Marsh*

Making an interesting comparison with the photograph on page 6, this is the view from platform 7 on the other side of the station but still at the western end. In afternoon summer sunshine, an unidentified 'Mogul' simmers as it pauses between duties. Elsewhere a period of calm ensues between train arrivals and departures. In this undated view, but probably from the late 1950s, note that the overall train shed has been dispensed with (in the 1932 rebuilding), leaving just the individual platform canopies – and part of the nearest one missing! The engine shed water tower can just be seen on the extreme right. *Crown Copyright, National Monuments Record*

The 10.50am two-coach train from Minehead arrives at the up main-line platform of Taunton station on 15 July 1958 behind No 5757. Although the branch service was usually worked by 2-6-2Ts, with freights normally in the hands of these more diminutive 0-6-0 pannier tanks, it was not uncommon for the service to be powered by such freight locomotives, especially if there had been a failure. Interestingly, however, No 5757 is wearing a 82D Westbury shedplate, rather than being a Taunton engine. Withdrawn from Westbury, No 5757 went on to work for London Underground, under the guise of LTE91. *H. C. Casserley*

SENGERS MUST
CROSS THE LINE
EFT BY MEANS
THE SUBWAY

14

Another view of No 46009 on 16 May 1979, with its consist of empty china clay wagons (see page 10), as the train leaves the station past the magnificent GWR 135-levered signal box and the highly attractive signal gantry.

The same view in 1999 has an altogether different atmosphere. Long gone are the delightful semaphores and the attendant signal box, and the trackwork has seen much rationalisation. Although a gantry remains, with its much shorter-bodied colour light signals, the appeal is not the same. On 22 August Virgin-liveried No 47854 – once named *Women's Royal Voluntary Service* – slows the ten-coach 1202 Paignton-Liverpool cross-country service for its Taunton stop. *Tom Heavyside/MJS*

A feature common to both of the last two views was Forty Steps footbridge, spanning the extensive trackwork to the south of Taunton station. This bridge gives superb views of trains travelling through the station, as exemplified in this view of No 47443 on a non-stop down express on 12 May 1979. Prominent above the train is the wonderful – and subsequently late-lamented – signal gantry, dismantled in 1985. Once such a common feature of our railway landscape, the loss of semaphore signals in general and gantries like this in particular has made the aesthetics of railway study that much poorer. Note that the engine shed still stands in this view, in the right distance, occupied by a couple of Class 08 shunters, a track machine and sundry freight wagons. To the extreme right, the 1896 station avoiding line swings out of sight. *Tom Heavyside*

Silk Mills Crossing is situated a mile or so south of Taunton, and with its four main-line tracks and sidings it was an ideal spot to watch expresses flash by. Displaying its Class A headcode, ex-GWR 'Hall' Class 4-6-0 No 7916 *Mobberley Hall* approaches the crossing, passing Blinkhorn Sidings, on a Paignton-Bristol (Temple Meads) train in 1961.

Eighteen years later the sidings are no longer in use and the nearest track of 1961 has been lifted. On 16 May 1979 No 47513 heads north with an unidentified shortened-rake train past the still intact bracket signals. Sadly, the scene has since drastically altered. *Peter Triggs/Tom Heavyside*

Norton Fitzwarren

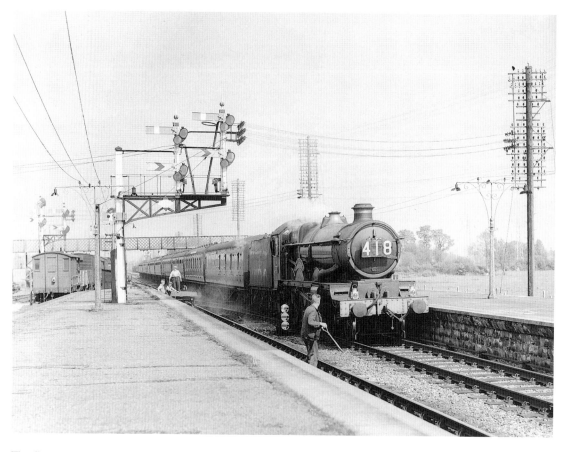

The first station west of Taunton, Norton Fitzwarren was the junction for both the Minehead and Barnstaple branches. Ex-GWR 'Castle' Class 4-6-0 No 5053 *Earl Cairns* enters the station from the east, but not for the branches or to stop, as it roars through with a Midlands-West of England express. The 'T'-sign at the platform end signifies the end of a permanent way restriction, but the gangers are right to be nervous of the thundering ten-coach express. To the left, a short freight train has the road from the station's No 19 ('up relief starter') signal for it to proceed towards Taunton.

At the end of the century the site has been transformed. Gone is all trace of the station, with only the two main lines and the Minehead branch (to the left in this view) still extant, together with the footbridge spanning them. Taunton Cider Co's private siding, to the left of the fence and trees, still has rails in situ but is closed. A First Great Western HST heads for Plymouth on 9 July 1999. *John Ashman FRPS, courtesy Mike Esau/MJS*

Originally the station had just two through tracks, from which the Barnstaple (from 1871) and Minehead branches veered at the end of the platforms (seen in the distance, to the right of the signal post). Known as Watchet Junction prior to the station being opened on 1 August 1873, the site was in open fields, well away from any sizeable habitation, so facilities were limited, although a hotel was provided. The roof of this – the imaginatively named Railway Hotel – can be seen just to the right of the station and above the goods shed on the right. A small waiting shelter adorns the down platform on the left, while even the main station building is of relatively meagre proportions. One presumes that no expresses were due in this posed, late-Edwardian view!

As part of the 1931 works to ease congestion in and around Taunton, the tracks were quadrupled through Norton Fitzwarren and the station complex was greatly enlarged, with four platform faces incorporating fast, slow and branch lines. Waiting areas were also suitably enlarged, as was the crossing footbridge, and a substantial GWR signal box was installed on the down side. In bright summer sunshine No 5024 *Carew Castle* has a clear road as it speeds through the station with an up express. *Lens of Sutton/John Ashman FRPS, courtesy Mike Esau*

This further view looking west towards the junction, undated but probably around the second half of the 1960s, shows the period after the station was closed to passengers on 30 October 1961. The station signboards have been removed and no doubt the Railway Hotel (right) will now attract far fewer travellers. Freight facilities were withdrawn on 6 July 1964.

Thirty-odd years later, again there is scant evidence of the former location. Only the Railway Hotel still stands, but on 9 July 1999 only as a boarded-up shell. *Lens of Sutton/MJS*

Bishops Lydeard

Once on the Minehead branch, the first station reached was Bishops Lydeard, 3 miles from Norton and actually some way from the village to which it referred. Like others on the branch, it was closed after the last services on 4 January 1971. In this first view from the mid-1970s, nature is attempting to re-colonise the area, with small bushes gaining a foothold in the 'four foot', grass beginning to carpet the platform and trees establishing a hold.

In earlier times a cattle pen stood on the far platform in the short bay; track was re-laid here in 1976.

Thirty years later the scene is, happily, much improved, and some of the successful transformation and development wrought by the West Somerset preservationists can be judged from this 1999 view. The old goods shed has been cleared of undergrowth and is now a small museum, and on both platforms waiting shelters, genuine GWR lamp posts, and shops have changed the whole ambience of the place. Despite appearances, this is the same vantage point as above, as the WSR has extended the up platform to cater for the much longer trains now operated for visitors. *Lens of Sutton/MJS*

Opposite At the other end of the same platform, the goods shed and waiting room buildings are seen just before services ceased. A rudimentary postbox clings to the waiting room wall, above the middle of the delightful period bikes, and evidence of occupation is provided by the neat appearance of the station platforms and buildings, including the lamp shed on the extreme left.

Again, the considerable progress by the preserved railway can be judged from this view from the summer of 1999. As well as a 'recreation' of the past, other facilities have been added for the visiting public; there has also been attention to the needs of operations, with a purpose-built water tower added at the far end. Also seen at that end of the platform is the old Station Master's house, now in private ownership. *Lens of Sutton/MJS*

Seen from close to the vantage point of the opposite page, but looking in the other direction, No 5548 pauses at the station on its way to Minehead with a train from Yeovil in 1959. Shedded at Yeovil at the time, the locomotive stayed there until withdrawal in June 1963. While long-distance through working was a feature of the line during its lifetime, this is evidence of a local variant. The leading coach, 6987, is part of a 'B' set with 6986, used regularly in and around the Taunton area. *Peter Triggs*

B & E R
—
To

Bishop's Lydeard.

The GWR Churchward-designed '45XX' 2-6-2Ts of 1906 were a mainstay on passenger turns for many years, work later being undertaken by the more modern '4575' Class variant. On 26 February 1960 one such, No 5543, enters the station with the 1.40pm four-coach Minehead-Taunton service, welcomed by just a small handful of intending passengers. Inroads were being made into the Class at this time and No 5543 lasted just five more months. Prior to 1906 the train would have been at the nearer platform, as the loop line on which the train is running and its platform were not brought into use until that time.

The emerging West Somerset Railway is on the scene in the 'interregnum years' of the mid-1970s, but it is still early in the preservation story and the volunteers have yet to exert a major influence on the station. There is a forlorn and lonely feel to the place, which is perhaps understandable, with the main efforts being expended further towards Minehead.

Twenty-five years or so of further progress is shown to advantage on 9 July 1999 as visiting ex-GWR 2-8-0T No 4277 enters the station with the 1400 service from Minehead. With platforms cleaned and resurfaced, station buildings restored to even beyond their former glory and the presence of flower beds and hanging baskets, the whole creates an attractive 'lived-in' atmosphere. Once a rusting Barry Scrapyard hulk, the superb restoration of No 4277, funded by owner Peter Best, can be well judged from this view. *John Spencer Gilks/Lens of Sutton/ MJS*

An extremely poignant picture: the date is 2 January 1971 and locals mix with enthusiasts, volunteers and general visitors to witness the passing of the last passenger train on the Minehead branch. The sad expression of ex-Ffestiniog Railway volunteer Robin Butterell seems to say it all! The gentleman on the tracks appears to be checking his cine camera – where is that film now? – but elsewhere there are precious few cameras to record the scene. Sadly, the last train to Minehead was made up of the usual DMU – no special celebrations for this service – and BR began the recovery of equipment, including the camping coaches, the very next day! *Western Daily Press*

70/35/14 WITHDRAWAL OF PASSENGER TRAIN SERVICES TAUNTON–MINEHEAD

The Minister of Transport has given consent to the withdrawal of the rail service between Taunton and Minehead. At the time of going to press a date for closure has not been determined. A notice will be included in the October supplement to the Western Region timetable advising passengers to confirm train times before travelling, since the service could be withdrawn as from Monday, 5 October, 1970. Booking Clerks and others concerned are asked to note this possibility and to make special enquiries when dealing with passengers wishing to travel over this part of the railway.   PM 13/566

From a BR staff circular of September 1970

Judging by the slip-streaming smoke in this delightful view from around 1910, the down train entering the station is approaching at some speed, while the two-coach period train on the near platform, with a Dean clerestory-roofed coach at the rear, awaits the road towards Taunton. At this time, the section from here to the junction at Norton Fitzwarren was still single, not being doubled until June 1936 (BR singled it again in March 1970!). Period lamps proliferate and milk churns, enamel signs for Pears Soap, etc, an ancient weighing machine and the gateway in the up platform fencing all complete the scene.

By the mid-1950s there are only subtle changes, but the ambience is wholly different. In what appears to be warm summer sunshine, a sole lady passenger waits for a train to Minehead. Elsewhere the goods shed has lost its chimney, the station building has had its ashlar sandstone chimney stack replaced by a brick one, and the area is devoid of lighting, but the goods trolley still awaits custom! On the up platform what looks like a corrugated iron lamp room has been provided, and presumably the gap in the fencing has been plugged, with access to the

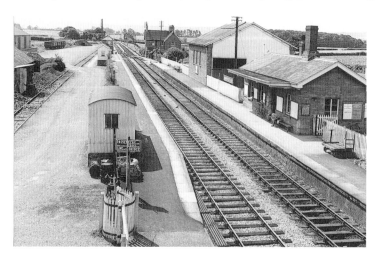

platform now by means of a kissing-gate. Note the goods siding to the left, installed around 1900 and here holding healthy stocks of various-sized lumps of coal. It ceased to operate from 12 August 1966. *Lens of Sutton/Joe Moss, Roger Carpenter collection*

The most noticeable change in the 20 years or so since the date of the previous view is the disappearance of the lamp room. The plugged gap in the fencing can still be made out by the bushy growth on the platform, but the coal siding has long gone. The space between the goods shed and waiting room on the down platform has been filled with the club room of the Taunton Model Railway Group, constructed in the 1970s. Other signs of the hand of the preservationists are in the repainted kissing gate, the re-emergence of enamel signs, the fact that the crossing warning sign now points the other way, and the 2-6-2Ts awaiting attention in the distance.

After another 20-odd-year leap, things have dramatically changed for the better. The kissing gate has been dispensed with, the fence gap making a return, together with disabled access; the goods shed has had a doorway and extension added to give entrance to and space for a museum; the station canopy has reappeared and plenty of seating has been provided; a purpose-built shop/cafe on the up platform has been in business since 1996; and there is now need to accommodate seven-coach trains. In July 1999 visiting BR Standard 2-6-0 locomotive No 76079 blows off while waiting to form a return service to Minehead. *Lens of Sutton/MJS*

In 1962 BR brought an element of dieselisation to the branch. Shortly after this a three-car DMU set pauses with a Minehead-Taunton service. The general run-down can be judged by the unkempt flower-bed on the far platform and the untidy chalked notice outside the waiting room on the right, but otherwise the station itself is still in creditably clean order.

A decade or so later, the preservationists have arrived. A 'Prairie' tank stands in the distance, awaiting its turn for attention, while elsewhere an attempt has been made to create some atmosphere to satisfy visitors in the period before the station can be properly dealt with. The 1906-vintage, 33-lever signal box still looks in good shape, considering that it closed in March 1970.

The station was re-opened to passenger services from 9 June 1979. Lavish attention has now been given to it and 20 years later, as well as period artefacts, the two staff members in appropriate costumes truly go a long way to restoring authenticity. Note the up waiting room nestling up to the 'new' shop/cafe and the extension of the platform past the signal box, and also that the goods shed siding is now only accessed from the down line, the previous crossover to the up line being severed. *Crown copyright, National Monuments Record/Lens of Sutton/MJS*

Crowcombe Heathfield

The first view shows Crowcombe as it was in 1966, without the 'Heathfield' appendage that was dropped from the original station name in 1889. Providing a passing place on the single-track line, it was a modestly adorned affair; in company with Blue Anchor, it was the only station on the branch not to have been graced with a goods shed. Opened in 1862, Crowcombe was, like Bishops Lydeard, a one-platform affair, this time on the up line, with the passing loop and signal box added in 1879 and the second platform in 1891. A porter's trolley stands abandoned by the gents' toilets, telephone bells adorn the wall and a Wickham trolley stands in the short siding. This siding was the terminus for stone from the nearby Triscombe Quarry. New houses now cover the site of the stone crushing plant.

On the face of it relatively little has changed, but there are numerous detail alterations. Perhaps most obvious is the renaming of the station to its original full length, reflecting the name of the area, rather than indicating a closeness to the village of Crowcombe, which is some distance from the station. The telegraph pole by the old nameboard has gone, with a lamp standard – from Tiverton Junction station – sprouting near to the spot; the short siding has been lost; the signal bracket on the left has changed its supporting post from metal to concrete; there has been an addition to the up home signal bracket to cover bi-directional working; and the whole area has a totally new, cared-for feel. Note also how much the trees to the left have grown, while those to the right have been reduced. *Lens of Sutton/MJS*

This extremely pleasant posed view shows the station and staff around 1900, an era so different from that after the world was turned upside-down by the 1914-18 War. A simple wooden signal post with oil-lit spectacle dominates, and oil also fuels the station lights. What appears to be a staff of three, plus one other, pose for their portrait on either side of the ex-broad-gauge bridge rail on longitudinal baulks of timber. Opened as broad gauge, the branch was 'narrowed' to standard gauge at the end of October 1882.

By 26 February 1960 signalling arrangements have been changed, the station lights have disappeared and the ticket office has lost some of its hoardings. The stone-built goods office still stands, however, seen just to the left of the train. By this time, although not visible in this view, the platforms have their 1934 increased length to accommodate holiday trains, but staffing levels have been reduced. 'Pannier' tank No 5525 has arrived with the 2.50pm Taunton-Minehead train.

On 9 July 1999 bunker-first 2-8-0T No 4277 makes a superb recreation of the above scene, running as the 1605 Bishops Lydeard-Minehead service. The signal bracket has been recreated, albeit slightly further along the platform, replacing the metal post seen on page 29. The station building has lost a chimney, but has been reroofed and has regained noticeboard adornments. Lighting has also returned to the station, this time electrically powered. There is now also a small ground signal, seen just to the left of No 4277. *Lens of Sutton/John Spencer Gilks/MJS*

In a view further south along the platform and looking back to Minehead, 'Pannier' tank No 5504 trundles through the station on 26 February 1960 with a truly mixed freight; it would appear that it is an amalgam of two shorter trains, judging by the brake-van sandwiched in the centre. Like others of the class, No 5504 was in its twilight years, being withdrawn from Taunton shed seven months later. The signal box, built in 1879, was destroyed by fire on 5 March 1967 and demolished by BR.

By 18 July 1970, the date of the second view, there is a completely different feel. Gone is the signal box, its place being taken by nature's reclamation, a point echoed in the encroachment of grass along the platform surfaces. Swindon Inter-City Class 123 DMU unit No 509 accelerates through the empty platforms with a 1A46 1300 (SO) Minehead-Paddington holiday train.

Once more the preserved railway has worked wonders on this isolated branch-line station. The signal box was replaced in the late 1980s by a much more attractive design than the original, the shell coming from Ebbw Vale Tinplate Works, being the former Ebbw Vale Sidings South box, and the frame from Frome North Junction box. There is now a waiting room with canopy on the down platform, and the undergrowth has been tamed, although a pleasant carpet of grass still decorates this side. The previously mentioned lengthening of the platforms can be seen from this view, with concrete facing taking over from the earlier brickwork. *John Spencer Gilks/Hugh Ballantyne/MJS*

These three views from the up platform, looking towards Bishops Lydeard, again show the highly impressive transformation wrought by the present WSR. The first was taken during the later days of BR control. In a semi-neglected state, only the presence of the semaphore signals at the platform ends and the bike leaning by the signal box steps give any clue that trains are still running. The design of the box was similar to those at Stogumber and Dunster. Once more the extension to the platforms can be seen just past the box. This point, at some 410 feet above sea level, is the highest point of the branch, with trains from Taunton having to climb continuously for some 6½ miles. The sharp change in gradient, from 1 in 81 to level through the station, can be seen as the tracks disappear under the bridge.

British Railways has gone by the date of the second photograph, but the preservationists have yet to appear. Not only are the trackwork and platforms being overtaken by greenery, but the space where the box was, in direct line with the tall tree, has been completely camouflaged. The station name-board on the left is bereft of information and signalling has been dismantled.

On 9 July 1999 it hardly seems the same place! A supreme example of what can be achieved with vision and effort, the station has sprung back to life, with the standards of restoration not only being extremely pleasing to the eye, but worthy of any competition for 'best kept station'. Indeed, this was borne out in 1985, when the station did in fact win the ARPS Award. *Lens of Sutton (2)/MJS*

Stogumber

Apart from the headboard on the locomotive, this peaceful country branch-line scene would be hard to date precisely. In early days of preservation, on 7 October 1976, ex-Torbay Steam Railway 0-6-0PT No 6412, complete with 'Flockton Flyer' headboard and splasher nameplate, climbs the 1 in 68 towards Crowcombe with a single ex-GWR Fruit D van, during filming sessions between Williton and Bishops Lydeard for Southern TV's series of children's programmes bearing that title. Transferred to the WSR on 25 March 1976, the locomotive had been out of service for much of the summer through damage to off-side piston, cylinder head and connecting rod. The only remaining substantial Stogumber station building stands in the distance.

A view from slightly closer to the station shows what improvements the railway has achieved over the ensuing 23 years. In July 1999 the area is free from unwanted undergrowth, the station waiting shelter and platform surface have been replaced and the brick building now houses a small shop. The old cattle dock on the right has been cleared, but in this isolated location there is unlikely to be a call for its re-introduction! *James Besley/MJS*

Here the original one-platform arrangement sufficed, and not long after closure of the branch the station stands in sweet repose, the trackbed prey to the advancing greenery. The simple wooden structure is under attack from brambles, and the distant track is already disappearing under grass. Note that the 'Beware of Trains' sign on the left appears to be warning pedestrians leaving the railway, as it stands by a gateway hidden by the left-hand tree.

Once more the 'present' scene is one of happy transformation. On 28 July 1999 a hot sun shines and a young family welcomes the shade from the waiting shelter. The new warning sign is now appropriately positioned, the crossing from the road approach is properly boarded, and the rotting platform timbers have been replaced by more durable substances. Note the period-style lamp standard on the left, complete with the station name on the glass. *Lens of Sutton/ MJS*

G W R
Newport to
Stogumber

The isolated nature of Stogumber station can be well judged from this view from the other side of the Doniford Stream valley. The road to the left leads to the village, but this is a mile or so away up a steep hill. Seen probably in the early 1930s, a Camping Coach stands perched by the road underbridge, while to the left of the station itself is the rather more substantial goods shed. The substantial building seen by the roadside was The Railway Inn, complete with skittle alley.
MJS collection

This view looking back towards Crowcombe is undated, but is probably in the post-1962 period, before yellow front-ends replaced the attractive 'whiskers' as warning on BR's non-steam traction. In late afternoon sunshine a three-car Class 120 DMU set leaves the station and heads south-east with a service for Taunton. To the left is the short siding to the goods shed, housing an old milk tank converted to supply drinking water for both station and camping coach, while the brick station building is on extreme left, complete with a row of five fire buckets.

Seen at a similar time of day in the summer of 1999, the station again exudes the air of volunteer care and attention, as a group of visitors from the nearby Bee World await the next train for Minehead. Note the coach in the same spot as in the photograph on the previous page, but this time not available for 'campers'. Like its twin at the platform end, the lamp bears the station's name on its glass. *Crown copyright, National Monuments Record/MJS*

This further undated view, but probably just prior to the First World War, shows the wooden extension to the platform, where the staff are standing, which was added in the early 1900s, and gives a fascinating glimpse of the station's past. Literally in the middle of nowhere, this tiny country halt, cut into the hillside, had a staff of three until 1933, when the post of Station Master was lost; one wonders how it could ever have justified the numbers. The fourth person in this view is perhaps a visitor or relief worker, but the gentleman by the building on the right, with his waistcoat and watch chain, is obviously of most importance as they all pose for their portrait. The building is attractively decorated with horizontal 'piping', while the platform is adorned with large oil lamps. The trackwork appears to again be sleepered in broad-gauge style and perhaps the securing of the rails is as seen at Crowcombe on page 30. Note the signal box, a structure not often seen in photographs as it was taken out of use in April 1926 and replaced by ground frames. The goods shed, containing a 2-ton crane, remained in active service until 19 August 1963, being demolished two years later.

The contrast at the end of the century is dramatic. On 28 July 1999 a party of children from Bee World makes a complement of passengers that would have gladdened the heart of any operator in pre-closure days. Prolific verdant growth largely hides the station building on the right, with the station nameboard also struggling to be seen. *WSR collection/MJS*

Williton

Situated just off the A39, Williton is a little over half way on the journey up the branch from Norton Fitzwarren and, strategically, is second only in importance to Minehead. Looking back towards Stogumber on 18 July 1970, we see 'Hymek' D7026 passing under the A39 road bridge and slowing as the driver exchanges single-line tokens with the signalman. The train is the 0620 (SO) Oxford-Minehead summer Saturday service bringing holidaymakers to the seaside in the last year of the branch's life. Although 22 years since nationalisation, there are still many ex-GWR features on display, including oil lamps, platform seating and station and signal box architecture. When the station opened in 1862, the main road ran across the tracks on the level, where the 'Hymek' is seen, the overbridge not being built until 1873, then rebuilt as seen here in 1952. It would seem to be wide for a single track and, indeed, previous operation saw two tracks under it until March 1967.

We next move into the early 1970s and all trappings of a live railway have gone. The station is bereft of life and the lamps have gone, as has the signal box nameboard; only the 'Beware of Trains' notice remains. Ivy is claiming the waiting room, and grass is sprouting quickly.

Once more, in 1999 the achievements of the present railway are self-evident. Now very much alive, the station oozes confidence and welcome, with the placing of period artefacts such as trolleys, milk churns, reproduction gas lamps and a sign for 'Park Drive Plain Cork Tipped' at '5 for 4d' making for a very attractive proposition. No doubt the 'Fresh Kenco Coffee' is very welcome to many travellers breaking their journey here. *Hugh Ballantyne/Lens of Sutton/MJS*

Although undated, the period is still in steam days, as witnessed by the water column standing between the tracks. With semaphores at danger in both directions, an air of calm pervades the station.

In early days following closure the scene is beginning to change. The water column has gone, as has the oil lamp on the near platform and the hedgerow bordering the far platform, all 'compensated' for by the arrival and proliferation of bramble and ivy. The semaphores still stand but the attendant wires along the platform frontage have gone.

As seen in the summer of 1999, those signal wires have been replaced, the fencing has been repaired, lighting has been positioned to cover more of the station than before and there has been extensive development to the left. A young lad who could almost pass for a street urchin from Dickens's day shows intense interest in No 50149, one of the railway's preserved main-line diesels, while beyond the engine repair shop gives cover to the staff and volunteers working on the new line's motive power. *Lens of Sutton (2)/MJS*

Like others on the branch, Williton station was originally constructed with just one platform – the down one, seen here. The second platform, together with passing loop, signal box and footbridge, were added in 1871. Seen first in the early 1960s, the footbridge that replaced the GWR covered original here frames the view of the down waiting room and booking office. The early morning sun picks out the clean lines of the goods shed and passenger facilities, making, with the water column in the foreground, an attractive portrait.

By the end of services on the branch, the bridge had been

demolished, leaving passengers/ pedestrians to brave the traffic on the level crossing at the end of the platform. On 28 July 1999 the station buildings are largely in original condition, other than detail differences and changes in signage, but elsewhere there has been more major development. The goods shed has had its previously open-topped doors extended to full height, there is a new extension at the far end and the previous open view to the distance has been filled in by the workshops and attendant sidings and stock. The workshops building is Grade II listed and came from Swindon Works in 1992. A ground disc has also been planted between the station tracks. *Lens of Sutton/MJS*

As so typical in photographs of Victorian/Edwardian times, the staff of Williton pose for their portrait, here in the shade from the bright summer sun afforded by the substantial signal box. The original covered passenger footbridge is well displayed here, as is the up waiting room. As can be seen when compared with the picture overleaf, after conversion from broad gauge the footbridge, originally built in 1871, was provided with a central support. One could almost be forgiven for thinking that 'Lipton's Tea' was the name of the station, given the size of the hoarding's lettering!

In hindsight, with this being merely a branch line without any express services, the provision of such a substantial footbridge does look a little 'over the top' and certainly, despite the obsession with health and safety later in the 20th century, the present operation by foot crossing seems perfectly adequate. There is obviously a far more open feel without the bridge, but other major changes, apart from the general smartening of the station by the preservationists, are the slewing of the up track to access the down line before the A39 bridge, and the provision of a semaphore signal on the platform on the right. Note the 'Brunelian' B&ER flat top to the chimney stack.

Lens of Sutton/MJS

Not a new view, but one that repays revisiting: the nearby Doniford Stream and its feeder tributary, the latter flowing under the railway, are not unknown to flooding, but thankfully the level of water seen here in 1877 is not the norm! Still in broad gauge days, the occasion is one of massive local interest, judging by the crowding not just on the platform end by the signal box, but also by the numbers of onlookers on the wooden footbridge. Many of these appear to be schoolchildren and perhaps they have been unable to reach school; similarly, the group of 'gentry' by the lamp standard on the up platform seem to be considering how they may reach the houses to the right. Interestingly, there do not appear to be tracks stretching away behind the train, an optical effect of the very short loop originally installed. This was lengthened in 1907 and again in 1937. Note that the up waiting room is a more primitive affair than as seen on the previous page. The stone building with the wooden vestibule on the left was the station lamp room.

As seen in the inter-war years, possibly post-1934, a substantial water tower has been erected; the footbridge has been replaced by a metal lattice type (during the 1920s) and moved to this end of the station buildings; the

signal box windows have been enlarged and the box now contains a 27-lever frame; a bracket signal has been installed on the right, together with catch points; a water column and winter brazier have been erected between the tracks; and on the left a single-line tablet-catcher has been provided. The footbridge was removed in the late 1960s. *Both Lens of Sutton*

By 13 June 1970, the last summer season of BR operations, there are obvious changes. Gone is the water tower, footbridge and twin track and, with the passing of steam, the water column has made way for that track reorganisation. The bridge carrying the railway over the Doniford Stream tributary, originally accommodating twin tracks, was rebuilt by BR in the late 1960s to the narrower width as seen in the right foreground. A DMU set enters the station with a service for Minehead, with the signalman about to exchange tokens, whilst a 'Hymek' diesel waits for the road with a Minehead-Paddington train. The distance still has an open, rural aspect, with just a single siding running into the goods shed yard at the far end of the station. This yard closed for business on 6 July 1964.

Six years on, with the preservationists now in charge, life is being restored to the station. On 9 September 1976 the 1500 ex-Minehead two-coach train has reached its destination and prepares to return to the terminus as the 1605. Note the huge water tank and its pedestal on the left; these subsequently went to Minehead – see the bottom picture on page 83.

Today, apart from the smartening of the station buildings, new structures, railway and non-railway, are the main features of change, at the same time depriving the view of its former rural feel. Industrial units, together with railway workshops and engine shed (visible beyond the signal box), crowd the country station in 1999. On 28 July the 1450 ex-Minehead disgorges its passengers, whilst 4-6-0 No 7828 *Odney Manor* has its headcode lamp removed before running round the train. The signal box is now the only remaining Bristol & Exeter Railway box still in full working order. *John Spencer Gilks/James Besley/MJS*

Like all preserved railways, visiting engines make for welcome additions to both public interest and indigenous motive power. On 13 July 1996, with owner Peter Best aboard, ex-GWR 'Heavy Tank' 2-8-0T No 4277 prepares to restart a Minehead-Williton and return special charter. The WSR was indeed fortunate to be the first railway to have the very powerful locomotive for a summer season, less than four months after being restored to life and running under its own steam for the first time for 32 years. Built in April 1920 as Works No 2857, the Churchward-designed locomotive spent the whole of its life in South Wales, largely using its impressive 31,450lb tractive effort moving coal and much of the time being an inhabitant of Aberbeeg shed. This fact is acknowledged by the 'ABEEG' painted on the frame just behind the buffer beam, in GWR tradition. The engine was an instant hit with loco crews on the WSR. *MJS*

G.W.R.

Williton
TO
Glastonbury
(Via Highbridge)

Doniford Beach Halt

A new facility opened in June 1988 and now known simply as 'Doniford Halt', the station, whose platform came from the closed Montacute station, serves visitors to the nearby beach and holiday camp. The line runs very close to the headland and is increasingly being threatened with encroachment of the sea undermining the approaches to the trackbed. Approaching the Halt on 13 September 1996, 2-6-2T No 4561 heads for Minehead, the proximity of the headland not being obvious from this angle. *Keith Lawrence*

A scene that would make aficionados of the line blink in astonishment! While there have been movements by the rail freight company EWS of stone for the Minehead seafront defences, a rake of Foster Yeoman locomotive and bogie stone hoppers on the branch is certainly highly unusual. In connection with the deployment of one of the Class 59s to Germany in 1997, driver training was required for the German drivers, but this could not be carried out over Railtrack metals. Foster Yeoman contacted the WSR, which was happy to lease its 21-mile route for the required training runs. These were supervised by the driver training division of National Power over the two days of 26/27 February 1997, and in this shot No 59004, the locomotive used for the trials, is seen passing the Halt on the first day, on its way from Blue Anchor to Williton. The trials were a great success for all concerned, earning valuable revenue for the railway. *Colin Marsden*

Watchet

Once the terminus of the line from Bishops Lydeard, Watchet was, with the rail-served harbour, a strategic point on the branch. With the opening of the line through to Minehead in 1874 and the later run-down in harbour tonnage, some of this importance was lost, but the goods shed and sidings still saw profitable business well into the post-nationalisation era. This view, possibly from the early 1950s, shows the always-limited passenger facilities and cramped layout.

Never possessing more than a single track through the station, passenger, freight and local shunting duties all had to co-exist; this was no place to experience timetable delays. The footbridge marked the boundary between the original branch and the 1874 Minehead Railway Co extension.

Sadly, the rail link to the harbour has long gone and, apart from the presence of the 1862 goods shed, closed to freight on 19 May 1965 and now home to the Watchet Boat Museum, there is little evidence of its prior existence. On the present WSR, however, all the buildings are extant, with only the ex-GWR seat missing from the earlier scene.
Lens of Sutton/MJS

A view looking the other way, back towards Williton, in the 1950s shows 0-6-0 pannier tank No 5779 involved in shunting duties. The box van is probably on its way from Minehead with a load of fish and the oil tank is presumably empty and being shipped back through Taunton, for re-filling. Some of the extent of the railway's presence here can be judged from the two further box vans seen just ahead of the locomotive, plus the loading gauge, both on the harbour's lower level, while the siding in front of No 5779 ran as a long headshunt, with the weighbridge seen ahead of the locomotive and a trailing connection down to the harbour lines. The harbour ceased railway functions on 19 May 1965.

In the summer of 1999, with part of the old railway land being given over to car parking, it is hard to visualise there being enough land to support the siding seen above. There has been much new development in the area on the left, in contrast to the continued presence of the corrugated hut on the platform. *Joe Moss, Roger Carpenter collection/MJS*

Above These two delightful and fascinating views show past operations at the harbour. In the first, something of the gradient up to the 'main' line can be estimated from the obvious slope up to the houses and church on the extreme left. In a view from around 1935, the four-wheeled, five-plank wooden wagons have obviously brought produce from all manner of sources, carrying, in addition to GWR, company initials SR, LMS, NE and LNW. Note the steamship in the harbour, the railed steam crane and the complete absence of people along The Esplanade. *Peter Treloar collection*

Below From a much earlier period and still in broad gauge days, Bristol & Exeter Railway 4-4-0ST No 74 stands on the turntable in 1872, posed with its crew for their photograph. Built in 1867 and fitted with a cab sheet, it is a fascinating example of early locomotive design. There were many odd-looking engines on the GWR broad gauge, with numerous builders being involved; although the builder of No 74 is unknown, the locomotive shares many details with other B&ER engines, not least the large steps to the footplate. Beyond, the railway runs on to the Eastern Pier, with the harbour breakwater on the left. On the extreme left of the view, the terminus of the West Somerset Mineral Railway can just be seen, situated at the end of the Western Pier. *Peter Treloar collection*

```
┌─────────┐
│  4237   │    G.W.R.
└─────────┘
         TO
WATCHET
```

In the early 1950s we may have been emerging from post-war austerity, but cars had not yet usurped trains and our railways still employed thousands of staff who cared for their charges. A certain amount of 'TLC' has obviously gone into the up-keep of Watchet station in this view, with the tidy appearance of posters, buildings and permanent way and the complete absence of litter.

Thankfully the WSR is continuing this tradition and has even advanced it with such things as hanging baskets. On 28 July 1999 the scene is one of quiet enjoyment for travellers and a pleasant environment in which to wait for trains. Changes to the scene are few, with the new lamp standard on the left, the shortened chimney stack in the centre, and the altered bridge parapet on the road bridge in the distance being the most noticeable. *Joe Moss, Roger Carpenter collection/MJS*

These three views vividly mark the passage of time at Watchet. Frustratingly, the right-hand poster date is obscured by the bridge pillar in the first, but it is estimated that the view is from the late 1950s. All the railway infrastructure is still in evidence, including the station gas lamp and the goods shed siding and loading gauge in the distance; with the left-hand poster advertising a Day Excursion to Weston-Super-Mare, the station is obviously still open.

The second view self-evidently dates from between closure and restoration, with the siding land already taken and building under way on this and adjoining land, beyond the goods shed. With grass and nettles once more colonising, the station looks forlorn, but interestingly a 'SW' ('sound whistle') notice for a footpath that crosses the line has appeared since the first image.

There is still verdant growth in the summer of 1999, but it is now largely grass and flowers and tolerated to add beauty to the end of the platform. A lick of paint, restoration of lighting, appropriate notice boards and disabled access all add to a more welcoming scene.
Lens of Sutton (2)/MJS

As seen before, visiting locomotives can add real variety and appeal to a railway, especially when the engine concerned is a famous one. On 21 July 1992 one such, 4-4-0 No 3440 *City of Truro*, the first locomotive to break the 100mph railway speed barrier, makes a fine sight leaving the confines of Watchet station with the 1555 Bishops Lydeard-Minehead service. The engineman, no doubt proud of being on the footplate of this honoured engine, rests briefly from his labours, casually leaning on the cab rail to enjoy the sunshine. Note on the left the goods shed facade much as it was in BR days, but with evidence of an altered doorway.
Tom Heavyside

One feature of the area around Watchet that is probably lost on the vast majority of visiting travellers is the prior existence of another railway. The West Somerset Mineral Railway ran to Watchet, West Quay, from Brendon Hills Iron Ore Mines, transporting iron ore to waiting ships. Although it closed in March 1910, there are still traces of it visible for those who know what to look for, such as this part of the old trackbed near Watchet now used as a public footpath. On 13 August 1962 0-6-0PT No 7713 crosses the alignment with an up freight on the approach to a once active siding to a paper mill, a footplateman precariously perched above the unguarded drop. The siding was removed in 1967. *Sydney Leleux*

Washford

After Watchet the railway swung sharply inland, once more meeting up with the A39 trunk road at Washford after negotiating the 1 in 74/92 Washford Bank. Ordnance Survey maps mark the spot where the two meet with the word 'Inn'. This hostelry, The Railway Hotel, is seen here on the right in a view from the late 1930s, as an unidentified '4575' Class locomotive enters the station with a Taunton-Minehead four-coach train. The smartly painted gate guards the crossing and entrance to the goods yard, which is behind the photographer to the left. Note the automatic tablet catcher to the left of the engine and the warning notice: 'Vehicles must stand clear of all railway lines when the crossing gate is closed'. *J Scott-Morgan, Roger Carpenter collection*

Looking in the opposite direction, this is the station that the above train is approaching. In around 1951 0-6-0 No 2268, with number on both buffer beam and smokebox in GWR and BR styles, pauses with a freight from Minehead. The diminutive signal box on the left is still open and may well be about to give assistance to shunting manoeuvres involving the wagons on the right; it closed on 24 August 1952. Two bicycles lean against the station wall, presumably not belonging to the elderly couple about to enter the waiting room! *Joe Moss, Roger Carpenter collection*

In a similar fashion to Watchet, Washford had a single platform without the benefit of a passing loop – although no doubt the goods shed track could be used in emergencies. Seen in around 1910, the station platform is lit for most its length by lamps and is adorned with flower beds and small trees, but a change of architectural style is evident. The extension from Watchet to Minehead was constructed by The Minehead Railway Co, opening on 16 July 1874. The whole area, including the goods shed with its ecclesiastically windowed extension, is clean and well cared for and the period picture is completed by the wooden ladder against the station wall, the goods wagon and cart, the flimsy looking wicker animal cage and what appears to be a primitive chocolate vending machine.

By the time of the second view, around 1958, the goods loading stage has been cut back and the trackwork altered slightly, and the goods shed chimney and cattle pen have gone, as have the old platform lamps and flower beds and some of the trees in the left distance. The short stub siding to the right also looks as though it has not been used for some time. Note that the 1934 extension to the platform now takes it way past the goods shed.

Once again the preservationists have made great strides in both smartening the site and recreating something of the past. Happily the small signal box has survived, although no longer in common use, and the whole station area looks much as it did one hundred years ago, with only detail differences. The greatest change has been the demolition of the goods shed and the total reorganisation of the trackwork and sidings. Double gateways now control access to the goods yard across the 'live' railway. *Lens of Sutton/Joe Moss, Roger carpenter collection/MJS*

Above Coming forward to the early restoration period, the station as it was taken over by the volunteers is seen on 23 March 1977. Pannier tank No 6412, with its short six-wheeled coach, has made the run from Minehead and is about to set off for the rest of the journey to Bishops Lydeard, to collect stock for the Somerset & Dorset Railway Trust, with a lamp headcode appropriate to a pick-up or branch freight train. Note that the new track alignment in the goods yard is already in position and now only awaits ballast. *James Besley*

Opposite Reverting back to much earlier in the 20th century, a collection of early 1927 travellers make ready to board the train arriving for Minehead. The porter strides briskly forward, presumably in readiness to open doors, while the little boy watches intently but clings to his father's hand. Evidently in summer, they are perhaps a family of holidaymakers about to spend the day at the seaside. Hauled by an ancient, outside sprung GWR 'Metro' Class 2-4-0T locomotive, in its last year on the branch, the coaches still bear destination boards and may well have come from beyond Taunton. Interestingly, the goods platform has seen a brick extension, a development that was reversed in later years.

Washford is now the venue for the Somerset & Dorset Railway Museum. Although the Minehead branch had no connections with the S&DJR, supporters of that line have amassed a highly creditable collection of artefacts and have made this part of Somerset their own. Superbly renovated freight stock stands in the freshly ballasted sidings. Note how the country feel of the area is dramatically changed with the loss of the once majestic trees. *Lens of Sutton/MJS*

G. W. R.

Washford

In about 1958 the goods shed and its siding are still extant, but there is obviously not as much traffic as of yore, judging by the grass between the tracks and the firmly closed door. Closure of the facility came on 6 July 1964 after a life just ten days short of 90 years. There is sign, however, of re-sleepering and fresh ballast on the running line.

By 20 June 1977 the goods shed has gone and work is under way on building its successor, whilst S&DR Trust engines and freight stock stand out in the open. The preserved line's two-car Park Royal DMU set, painted in maroon and cream house colours and comprising coaches 50413 and 56168, restarts the 1705 Williton-Minehead shuttle, the design of the unit giving superb front views to a few lucky passengers. Note the dilapidated state of the fencing and the need for some assiduous weeding.

On 28 July 1999 the scene is again transformed. The 1989 workshops and museum are well established, the sidings complete and properly controlled, and platform and fencing restored and cared for. The signal post is an ex-LSWR type with a 'backing' arm as seen at several points on the old S&DJR and the gates are from Edington Junction, an ex-S&DJR location. A pleasing vista and a credit to the railway. *Joe Moss, Roger Carpenter collection/Tom Heavyside/MJS*

Blue Anchor

On the final approach to Blue Anchor station from Washford, the track opens out from single to double track to create a passing loop in the station confines. On 18 July 1970, still controlled by an ex-GWR lower-quadrant signal, 'Hymek' D7026 approaches the limit of this double-track as it leaves the station with the 1025 Minehead-Paddington train. The ramp of the down platform can just be seen on the left. There is a dispute over whether the station was originally called Bradley Gate or Blue Anchor Excursion Platform, but certainly the current form was listed in early timetables. There is also uncertainty as to whether the somewhat enigmatic name celebrates a local inn or the adjacent bay; the nearest village, Carhampton, is a mile or so away. *Hugh Ballantyne*

Looking from that platform ramp, we see 0-6-0PT No 6412 propelling its five-coach load away from the station on 1 April 1976 past that same signal. Having run round its train, the slightly unusual sight of the locomotive pushing rather than pulling will only be as far as the points, after which the train will reverse into the down platform for eventual return to Minehead. *James Besley*

Another view of the 1555 Bishops Lydeard-Minehead train of 21 July 1992, hauled by celebrity locomotive No 3440 *City of Truro*. The train has now reached Blue Anchor and as it slows for the station stop the fireman is ready with his single-line token, prepared for the changeover for the next section at the end of the platform. Note the abandonment of the ugly concrete-posted lighting, with a recreation gas lamp in place, now electrically controlled. The attachments hanging from these posts were part of the pulley system, used during the period of pressurised oil lamps for lighting. *Tom Heavyside*

The first view is possibly from around 1920, but certainly post-5 January 1904, the date that the down platform on the left, the loop, signal box and crossing gates were brought into use. Station Master and porter pose for their portrait during a quiet spell at the station. Note the strangely shaped building at this end of the quartet of structures on the up platform, forming the ladies' toilet, and the provision by the Minehead Railway Co, as at Washford, of flower beds on the platform.

The passage of time, through nationalisation and into closure, has not been kind to the station, as seen in the second view, from around 1972. The basic infrastructure remains, but the previously well-tended garden features have become a wilderness and the earlier fencing has been lost completely. At this stage the crossing gates stay stubbornly closed.

Once more the WSR has brought the station back from the dead. Freshly painted barge boards set off a now well-kept and attractive facility, and one for which the railway does not have to make any apologies to its visitors. Again, happily, so much of the infrastructure has survived to allow the recreation, with only the up platform shelter having been rebuilt from the original in this July 1999 view. *Lens of Sutton (2)/MJS*

A view from the early afternoon in the mid-1930s sees a crowd of holidaymakers waiting for their train to Minehead. Perhaps they are staying in the fairly new holiday accommodation seen in the distance and, having spent the morning on the beach at Blue Anchor, are about to spend the afternoon in the town. Note the provision of oil lamps on the station at this point and even a public telephone, denoted by the sign on the left-hand waiting shelter, as well as the 1934 extension to the up platform.

By May 1960 the clearance of flora from the rear platform edges and the disappearance of the shapely lamp standards gives a far more open aspect to the station, the slightly less attractive atmosphere not helped by the wet weather obviously recently endured. 'Prairie' tank No 4157 pauses to pick up its complement of passengers for Minehead with a train from Taunton.

Period lamps are back and arboreal growth has helped to soften the hard edges from the previous scene. The sun has also reappeared in this view from July 1999, aiding the station's inherent attractiveness. The 1989 redesign of the up waiting room, to replace the rotting original, is well seen from this angle. *Lens of Sutton/Joe Moss/MJS*

One of the more attractive views at Blue Anchor is that towards Minehead, past the signal box and the beach area. On 20 August 1962 2-6-2T No 5563 slows to exchange single-line tokens as it crosses the B3191 road and enters the station. Seen here without identifying shedplate, No 5563 survived longer than many of its sisters, being transferred late in life to Yeovil shed and finally being withdrawn in October 1964.

Little has changed by 18 July 1970, other than the removal of the loading gauge by the beginning of the single track on the left. A twin three-car DMU pairing enters the station, with a Class 116 set leading, forming the 1120 Minehead-Taunton service.

The 'flares' give the game away that the third photograph is from the mid to late 1970s! Rugby shirts and T-shirts complete the outfits in this delightful period scene, dating from August 1977, as pannier tank No 6412 approaches the station with a train from Minehead. Other than the disappearance of a GWR notice, again little has changed. *Sydney Leleux/Hugh Ballantyne/ Norman Kneale*

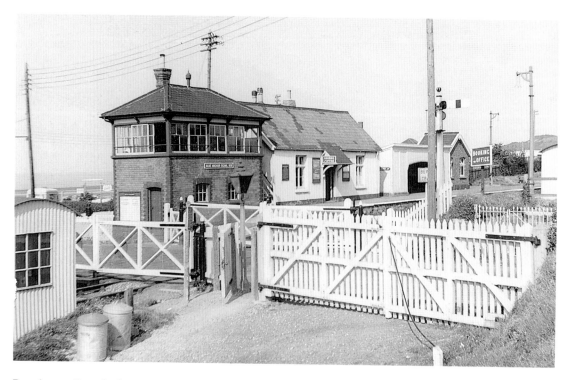

Running a railway is about far more than just the trains. All manner of ancillary operations are needed to support the smooth running of the services and perhaps none more so than signal boxes. Here the ex-GWR box at the western end of Blue Anchor station is seen to advantage in the summer sunshine of 1 July 1965. Controlling the crossing as well as the trains themselves, the job of the signalman was/is very important, requiring trustworthy and alert members of staff.

The same scene in 1999 is little changed, other than detail differences on the station buildings, the new down platform waiting room and the alterations to the entrance to the foreground area. Note the continued existence of the lamp hut, and that a strategic 'Beware of Trains' notice has been placed on the box by the WSR. *Richard Casserley/MJS*

A view not normally vouchsafed the public – the inside of a signal box. Attired in typical railway uniform – including waistcoat but without watch and chain! – the Blue Anchor signalman demonstrates the 'pulling off' technique to operate the semaphore signals and points on 20 August 1962. The handle of one bearing his coat, the short line of 17 levers stand ready to do their bit, while beyond is the large wheel that will open and close the road level crossing gates. The shelf over the window bears all manner of interesting items, including lamps, a teapot, a bucket and a box containing 'Kitchenware. No. 70 Sanican'! With a benevolent half-smile on his face, one can imagine that this man was popular with those who knew him. *Sydney Leleux*

In a present-day variant, volunteer and railway author and photo-grapher Richard Derry poses for his picture in the window of the box at Blue Anchor in September 1998. While no less dedicated than their forebears, the volunteer signalmen do not have to endure the weeks and months of often very lonely existence in all seasons and weathers. *Richard Derry collection*

Immediately on leaving the station on the journey to Minehead, trains pass close by the beach area. In August 1962 this is to the left, hidden by the holiday chalets in this view of 2-6-2T No 4128 restarting a Taunton-Minehead train. To the right is more holiday accommodation, in the guise of 1910/1914-vintage 6-berth camping coaches, and heads from these peer at similarly investigative faces in the train coaches. *Sydney Leleux*

A close-up view of two of those ex-GWR corridor 3rd Class camping coaches, seen here on 1 July 1965, presumably a hot day as all the drop-light windows are open. W9887W, withdrawn from normal service in 1956 and renumbered from 3639 in January 1957 when converted to camping coach use, was a real GWR remnant, being a 57-foot TK coach built in 1910. Beyond is W9889W, ex-2578, a 57-foot 'Multibar Toplight' eight-compartment corridor 3rd, built in 1914. Again condemned in 1956, it was converted, renumbered and initially sent to Marazion in Cornwall. Transferred to Blue Anchor in 1963, it remained with its two companions until the closure of the branch in 1971. At the time of this view, the coaches were less than watertight and they were removed to Dawlish Warren for repair. The siding on which they stand opened as a goods 'yard' on 1 April 1913, but closed on 19 August 1963; it is still connected to the running line in this view.

Thirty-four years later all three coaches are back, now providing volunteer accommodation, but despite evidence of the steps it is to be hoped that the nearest coach, No 3639 (ex-9887 seen above), is unoccupied, as it is certainly in need of some more serious renovation, which, happily, it is now receiving. At the time of this photograph in July 1999, the far two were outwardly in good shape and occupied. The siding connection was severed in 1976. Note the presence of the railway's trouble-shooting van. *Richard Casserley/MJS*

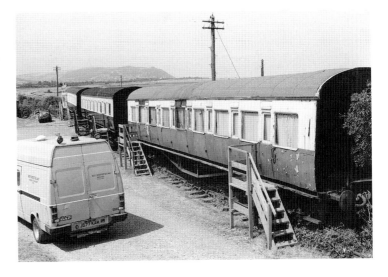

Dunster

As the single track from Blue Anchor makes the final approach to Dunster station, the line passes over the Dunster-Dunster Beach road at Sea Lane Crossing. In 1977 0-6-0 pannier tank No 6412, complete with buckets and fire-irons, slows for this level crossing, hauling a six-coach train from Blue Anchor to Minehead. Although now controlled by flashing lights, it is the only crossing on the branch to retain its keeper's cottage, now privately owned. This length of train was unusual at this time and was perhaps a stock movement. *Peter Triggs*

Dunster's slightly grandiose architectural style and the equally grand sweep of the approach drive, unusual for a small country station, owe much to the presence of Dunster Castle and the Luttrell family. Incumbent in the castle since 1376, the then residents were among the promoters of the Minehead Railway Co's extension from Watchet in 1870. Looking north-west towards Minehead in the 1950s, the driver of the coal lorry is about to leave his cab, perhaps to use the weighing scales standing by the wagons. Fertiliser was another regular inwards item and no doubt the goods van by the goods shed on the right has brought some into the yard. At the far end of the platform the all wooden ex-Maerdy signal box marks the re-arrangement of control following the 1934 doubling of the track from here to Minehead. For 60 years from 1874 a box had stood at the other end of the platform, although it was actually taken out of use in 1926, replaced by two ground frames.

By comparison the early 1970s view leaves much to be desired. The goods shed sidings have gone, as has the station nameboard, erected after the earlier view, and the trees behind the railings. Note the replacement by BR of the previous single semaphore with a double bracket, controlling the two tracks to Minehead.

Once again the restoration by the WSR has brought positive results, with a siding again running into the goods shed. Note how the rampant tree growth now shields the station from this angle. Beyond the West level crossing, at the far end of the station, the track to Minehead is now operationally and physically single, the previous up line having been lifted in 1977.
Lens of Sutton (2)/Richard Jones

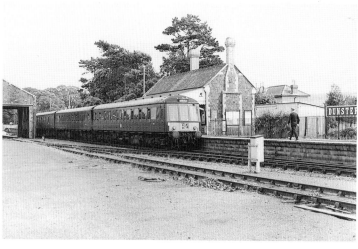

In this 29 April 1962 view of the station from the goods yard, all is still neat and tidy, although the flower beds planted when the station was opened have long since gone. The 1874 goods shed on the left is still in use (until 6 July 1964), posters still adorn the station walls and the gate to the Station Master's house looks to have been recently repainted. Note that the pressurised oil lamps are now not in use.

Just over a year later, on 3 July 1963, things remain unchanged. A three-car DMU set now handles much of the passenger duties and here leaves for its last stretch to Minehead. The site of the old signal box, on the end of the platform, can be seen through the open goods shed doorways.

Showing the success of restoration, it is almost as if the railway has never been away. On 4 September 1999 part of the WSR's own DMU fleet superbly recreates the earlier view on a Williton-Minehead service. The new fencing in the foreground does not look out of place in the period recreation with the original lamp post and station sign, and the platform trolley. *P. J. Garland, Roger Carpenter collection/R. C. Riley/ Richard Jones*

Once more looking towards Minehead, by 1 April 1976 the ex-BR signals have lost their arms as 0-6-0PT No 6412 coasts into the station with the 1600 service from Minehead. Note that the train has approached on the old main line and is negotiating the pointwork leading to the single track through the station.

This arrangement can be seen more clearly in the second view showing the Park Royal DMU set plus an additional coach arriving at Dunster on 12 August 1976. This is an unusual trio, but there were no steam locomotives available on this day! Note the ex-BR crossing warning signs still in use. *Both James Besley*

Minehead

The final approach to Minehead is a long straight section from the south-east, crossing the flat, former marsh area sandwiched between the A39 road and the shoreline. On 17 September 1964 a three-car DMU set approaches the terminus on the last leg of its run from Taunton as the 9.45am service. Nestled in the lee of the hill, the town is spread out before the train, with the station canopy just visible as a horizontal white slice in the centre distance. A horse pauses to give a cursory glance at the passing machine. Once only accessible by foot, this view can now be had from the new road approach to the town. *R. E. Toop*

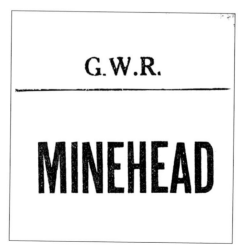

In the throat of the station approach the single line that has run from Dunster spread out to give access to platforms and sidings. Note that on 25 March 1976 there is no connection between the two tracks – any movement from one to the other had to be made via Dunster at this time! The maximum approaching train speed is clearly indicated on the left. We are in the early preservation era and No 6412 undertakes some shunting, with auto-coach 238, on loan from the Dart Valley Railway. The Park Royal two-coach DMU set stands in the main platform, while to both left and right of it stand steam locomotives. Elsewhere the scene has an uncluttered feel that would be largely lost as the railway develops. *James Besley*

SOUVENIR TICKET - WSR - SOUVENIR TICKET

WEST SOMERSET RAILWAY

1976 23 MARCH **1986**

TEN YEARS OF OPERATION

Minehead - Blue Anchor

Ticket valid for one Return Journey
on Friday 28 March 1986

CHILD   £0·90   № 0121

SOUVENIR TICKET - WSR - SOUVENIR TICKET

The first of these three views looking back towards Dunster from close to the platform end is dated around 1948, just into nationalisation, and the immediate impression is one of flatness and openness, with the reclaimed marshland stretching to the headland beyond Blue Anchor. '2251' Class 0-6-0 No 2213, no stranger to the branch, starts its journey to Taunton past the GWR lower-quadrant bracket signals in bright sunshine. To the left are the 1934 32-lever signal box, the water column, the siding starter signal and a tall water tower. Note also the gangers' hut nestling between the latter two. The signal box closed in March 1966, when the run from Dunster became operated as two single tracks (see the previous page).

Into preservation days, a morning departure from Minehead to Williton returns. With the absence of semaphores at the platform end, the openness is now more a feeling of dereliction. To the left, beyond the trees, the buildings of the Butlin's Holiday Camp, opened in 1962, can just be seen.

The surrounding topography cannot be altered, but with the growth of trees, the development of the 'marshland' and the 'TLC' lavished on the scene by the volunteers, the situation is drastically altered for the better. In the summer of 1999 not only have signals (from Newton Abbot station), box (from Maerdy) and water tower (from Pwllheli) been replaced, but there have also been additions of sidings on either side of the station. *Joe Moss, Roger Carpenter collection/James Besley/ MJS*

In the last summer of BR operation, signs of neglect are obvious in the weeds gaining a foothold on the platform surface and the lampless standards. On 18 July 1970, having arrived with the 0620 (SO) Oxford-Minehead train, D7026 runs round the stock ready to form the 1025 service to Paddington. At that time this was the only movement on that track each week. To the left, the track and connections to the old engine shed and turntable have been lifted, the former having been demolished and the site now becoming overgrown.

Seven years later life is being breathed back into the station and its surroundings. With increasing stock, both mobile and stationary, stabled on the left, No 6412, again with the 'Flockton Flyer' headboard, makes a spirited departure with its complement of holidaymakers and trippers on 20 June 1977. Note in the goods yard on the right track panels and two locomotive boilers awaiting their turn for attention. *Hugh Ballantyne/Tom Heavyside*

This view of the station, probably in the summer of 1948, gives a superb glimpse of the wide sphere of operation around the restricted terminus platforms at Minehead. The previously seen No 2213 here stands ready to leave with its train, as last goodbyes are said. At this time No 2213 was the one engine sub-shedded to Minehead. To its left the single-road engine shed can just be seen, while to the right a mixed goods train stands tarpaulined and ready. A '45XX' locomotive, presumably the goods engine, pauses in the goods shed doorway and the scene is completed by sidings, 6-ton crane and small cart. The town, with the church halfway up the hill, makes a fine backdrop.

The second scene is undated, but is probably from the 1950s and is undoubtedly a summer day, probably a Saturday, as the coaching stock on the left bears the legend 'Birmingham, Bristol, Taunton and Minehead'. The obvious length of this train and the quality of coaches clearly announces that it is not an ordinary branch train. 'Prairie' tank No 5157 stands with just such a train on the right, waiting to make its less hurried way to Taunton. It would be interesting to know why the young lad on the left is running with his fingers in his ears!

The same view in July 1999 shows a much more developed scene, with flower borders around the nameboard and elsewhere on the platform and attention paid to cleanliness and public perception in these image-conscious days. *Joe Moss, Roger Carpenter collection/Peter Treloar collection/MJS*

L. & N. W. RY.
Minehead

2nd - SINGLE   SINGLE - 2nd

Minehead to

Minehead   Minehead
Birmingham New St.   Birmingham New St.

BIRMINGHAM NEW STREET
via Bristol and Bromsgrove
For alternative routes see book of routes

(W)   43/3   Fare   43/3   (W)
For conditions see over   For conditions see over

3634   3634

This is another undated view, but probably again from the 1950s, as the small 'garden plots' have gone from around the lamp standards since the photograph on page 76. The station has had positive attention, however, as many surfaces appear to have been recently repainted, including the water tower and the end of the shed buildings on the left. On what looks to be late afternoon on a sunny spring day, a 'commuter' walks towards the train with her offspring, both hands laden with shopping. No 5504 simmers, awaiting the 'right away' for it and its five-coach train to leave for all stations to Taunton. This locomotive succumbed to withdrawal in September 1960, from Taunton shed.

The railway still has three sidings to the left, for stock storage, but the shed and turntable area has now largely been swallowed by a car park. The day may be dull in July 1999, but there are plenty of visitors thanks in no small part to the special charter train on the right. *Lens of Sutton/MJS*

The ubiquitous 'Flockton Flyer', behind No 6412, is seen again on 20 June 1977. Awaiting the time to leave, the locomotive receives plenty of attention. Note the twin 'WSR' headcode discs.

Nearly four years later there is little obvious change on the railway, but on the right the previous single-storey concert hall buildings have been swept away to be replaced by the 'Carousel' amusement arcade. On the goods shed approach siding, ex-BR shunter D2994 stands with another acquisition from British Rail, a former Mk1 coach. However, the centre of attention on Sunday 15 March 1981 is No 2996 'Victor' doing its best to impersonate a volcano as it starts the 1015 train to Bishops Lydeard. Originally built in 1951 for work in Margam steelworks, the locomotive transferred to the Austin (now Rover) works in Longbridge, Birmingham, in 1957, eventually arriving at the WSR in 1975. Having given valiant and sterling work on the railway, it was later again moved, this time to the Strathspey Railway in Scotland in 1988, and is now based at Shackerstone on the Battlefield Line in Warwickshire. To the left, the two-car Park Royal DMU set is reserve. *Both Tom Heavyside*

Above Comparatively speaking, there are relatively few views of the Edwardian railway at Minehead, so although published elsewhere it is pleasing to see again this train being loaded with all manner of bags and baggage and even, it would appear, a shrouded coffin into the nearest van. Elsewhere, doors stand open on the front coach to welcome the well-dressed ladies, with a clerestory-roofed coach behind. To the right, a sheeted freight train waits its turn for attention. Note that the station building is still in its original, un-extended condition, but that the 1905 second platform face, right, is now in use. *Lens of Sutton*

Above right This view of Minehead's engine shed is dated 15 July 1958. A relatively diminutive affair, it adequately served the needs of the branch, whose locomotives, apart from the freight stock, largely worked out and back from Taunton, receiving any servicing and/or attention at that town's much larger facilities. The water tower seen here replaced a bigger affair on four legs, provided when the shed first opened. The photograph was taken from the platform, so the close proximity to the station can be judged. The shed (which closed on 3 November 1956), sidings and turntable (seen below) were all swept away in 1966. *H. C. Casserley, courtesy Richard Casserley*

Right The depot's turntable was just off the left of the view above and is seen here in the mid-1950s. The original structure had been squeezed between shed and platform, but with the increase in train and motive power lengths, this newer 45-foot version was constructed in 1905. '43XX' Class 2-6-0 No 5325, of 82A Bristol (Bath Road) depot, has just been turned, having possibly arrived with a through train from the Midlands. The need to turn tender engines at Minehead certainly presented a potential problem, as the turntable was not quite long enough to accommodate them. Note the somewhat ingenious solution to this, by way of raised extension ramps at the rear of the table itself, holding the tender clear of the ground as the locomotive is turned. The ramps were not popular with engine crews as they tended to unbalance the locomotive on the table. The last locomotive to use the turntable was a surprising one – ex-LMS 'Pacific' 4-6-2 No 46229 *Duchess of Hamilton*, when she arrived for

display at Butlin's! Built in September 1917 and serving with the ROD in France when new, No 5325 was renumbered as 8325 from March 1928 to July 1944, when it was fitted with increased front-end weight, in an attempt to overcome flange wear on sharp curves. It was finally withdrawn in August 1957 from 83B Taunton depot and this visit to Minehead might have been in connection with the move to the new shed. *Peter Treloar collection*

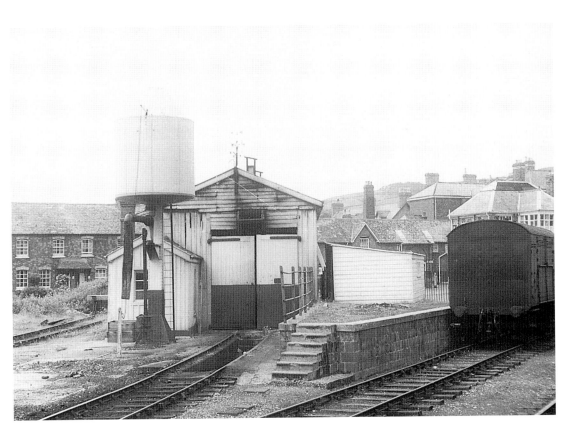

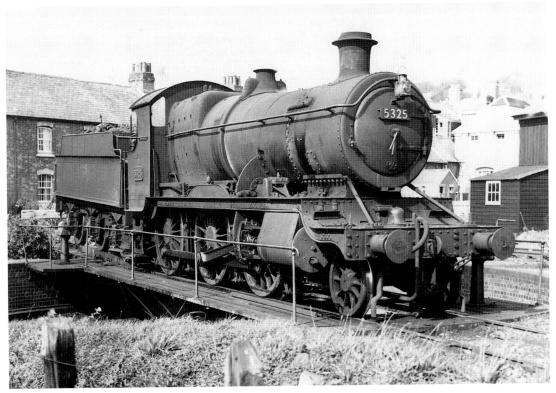

Despite the grass on the platform, this delightful picture demonstrates both the achievement and appeal of the restored West Somerset Railway. On 3 August 1987 2-6-2T No 5572, a visitor from Didcot for the season, with its number on the buffer bean in GWR tradition, gently brings its rake of coaches into the station in the warm sunshine before making its way as the 1405 service to Williton. The holiday crowd display their eagerness to sample the delights of their journey. To the right stands one of the railway's expanding collection of DMUs, awaiting its turn on duty. *MJS*

The first of these three views of the goods shed and yard was taken off-season in the very early 1960s. Pannier tank No 5798 shunts the yard with a healthy and varied collection of freight stock. Two box vans are sandwiched between steel-bodied 16T and wooden 10T wagons, while there are more both beyond and to the right. The rain pouring down, it is not surprising that there are no passengers to be seen! Freight facilities were withdrawn on 6 July 1964.

At 5.30pm on April Fool's Day 1976 the weather is again closing in, with mist descending over North Hill in the distance. Seen from a train in the platform, No 6412 stands with a short freight. Note the presence of the old goods dock on the right, but now without track or cattle pens.

By the summer of 1999 the preservationists have wrought many changes. A new workshop and water tower have been built; the goods dock has gone, giving room for more sidings; and the goods yard trackwork has been altered, to give a longer line to the goods shed. One of the line's 'Manors', No 7828 *Odney* Manor, stands 'ragged up' between duties, while one of the day's operating locomotives, BR Standard No 76079, visiting from the East Lancs Railway, has its smokebox door open for ash removal. *Joe Moss, Roger Carpenter collection/James Besley/MJS*

Another panoramic view of the terminus, which is just short of 188 miles from Paddington. On 15 July 1958 0-6-0PT No 5757 is the centre of attention for a little boy and his father as it waits to form the 1050 train to Taunton. Elsewhere, things are much as they had been for the period since enlargement in 1934, the only immediately noticeable difference being that the loco shed doors are closed, the facility no longer operational. *Richard Casserley*

This attractive and somewhat unusual view of No 2250 engaging in a spell of shunting with box vans is undated, but is possibly from the early 1960s. As much of the branch freight was in open wagons, this may have been a special delivery or collection, a possibility in view of the lamp headcode. To the left a '41XX' locomotive waits to leave with its train.

The second view, taken on 10 July 1957, shows 'Mogul' No 6327, of 82B Bristol (St Philip's Marsh), as a little 'over the top' in the way of motive power for this lightweight two-coach 1220 passenger turn to Taunton. The fireman spends a few minutes pushing coal towards the front of the tender, while the guard prepares to close the carriage door, perhaps unaware of the approaching lady behind him. *MJS collection/Frank Hornby*

As the 1950s progressed, road transport began to make real inroads into rail traffic throughout the UK. Minehead was no exception to this, and here we see a Taunton-registered Scarlet & Blue coach parked near The Strand, having brought a private party to the seaside just 11 days after the above photograph. Although the local roads were full of twists and turns, the relative comfort of these coaches and their greater flexibility over the railways made them increasingly popular. *Norman Simmons, Hugh Davies collection*

This is the view under the station canopy, looking out towards Dunster and points east between closure and occupation by the 'new' WSR. The car parking area to the left is fenced off from the running line, which, in common with much of the rest of the view, is succumbing to the onward march of grass and general weed infestation. Seemingly, the darker area under the canopy is not encouraging such growth.

Nearly 30 years later, in the summer of 1999, the position is happily one of restoration and prosperity. The station, which boasts the longest platform on any preserved railway in the UK, is once again bustling with activity, on and off the platform, with an added interest factor being the goods yard in full view of visitors and travellers. No 7828 *Odney Manor* on the left and coaching stock on the right wait their turn in serving the increasing numbers of visitors, while in between No 76079 has the ash of a day's work cleaned from the smokebox. *Lens of Sutton/MJS*

The first, undated, view, probably from the early 1960s, shows the terminus basking in summer sun in a quiet period between trains. Box vans stand on the line from the goods shed, while on the platform, a rudimentary postbox and two trolleys await custom. A solitary bicycle and broom lean against the station wall, enhancing the feeling of siesta.

By the date of the second picture the branch is now closed, station artefacts have gone or are in disrepair, track has been lifted and grass and weeds grow aplenty. The yard telegraph pole has also been dispatched, severing any previous communications links. On the street, at the end of the sole remaining line, an elderly couple look at the dereliction, perhaps mentally reliving earlier visits to the railway.

With the preservationists taking residence relatively quickly after closure, the station is structurally largely intact, with platform canopy and even the water fountain still extant. In July 1999 the scene is transformed. Posters are back on the wall, track is re-laid, engines Nos 4277 and D2271 stand waiting a call, and the whole exudes an air of care and attention. Note that the trees at the end of the tracks have not fared well, with the vista to the hill beyond now being clear. The very authentic-looking lights nestling under the canopy originated in Taunton station. *Lens of Sutton (2)/MJS*

In this scene 'from the street' in 1960, what appears to be an old auto-coach brings up the rear of a train in the platform, while on the left freight is assembled and sheeted ready for onwards transfer to Taunton and beyond.

During the closure period, the second view was taken on the same day as the centre picture on page 87, and provides a sad commentary on the mentality of careless abandonment. The track was truncated by BR to the previous run-round point in 1966, when the Minehead signal box was closed, but even that shorter length is now without a buffer stop, and although a replacement turn-out has been provided further up the platform, this end is still potentially dangerous.

Once more the 'present' scene shows a positive transformation. It is easy, after the event, to take for granted the often Herculean efforts by volunteers and the few permanent staff on our heritage railways, but when greeted by views such as this, they are all to be heartily thanked and congratulated. With Nos 4277 and D2271 in good shape and with the shop proudly advertised and paintwork gleaming, one can be excused for thinking that it was ever thus. Note the 'indenting' of the platform edge, to give clearance for some of the larger locomotives when negotiating the re-instated pointwork. The ticket office, on the extreme right, is a recent addition, incorporating parts from Cardiff Central station. *Joe Moss, Roger Carpenter collection/Lens of Sutton/MJS*

Looking at Minehead station in the last year of the 20th century, it is virtually impossible to imagine how it was originally built. A view from the turn of the 19th century shows just how much smaller and limited were the early facilities. Not that this seems to have affected traffic, judging by the crowd here present and the plethora of horse-drawn coaches. There is a long train in the station and, with the general finery displayed by both men and women, this is no doubt a very special party. Note the out-of-character pagoda-style corrugated iron hut addition to the station, added by the GWR, and the simple hoarding on the station railings to the extreme left advertising the Headland Hotel. The coach-and-four by the pagoda waits to start its run to Lynton.

Although it is perhaps difficult at first sight to appreciate that this is the same station, the entrance portico to the booking hall can be recognised as the original, together with the two windows to the left of it. The previous building finished level with the middle chimney stack, this being incorporated into the much fuller extension. When the building was extended, first in the 1920s, then again in 1934, the whole branch was upgraded. On 15 July 1958 the scene is much less frenetic than that above and, indeed, with the 'Oxford bags' on the gentleman studying the timetable to the left and the vintage Armstrong Siddeley car, the view could almost have been from between the wars.

Exactly 41 years later again the atmosphere had changed. The building survives, but the explosion of car travel is reflected in the provision of parking spaces and the Pay & Display control. Two chimney stacks have been reduced, the telegraph pole has gone, the building exterior is largely devoid of posters and the entrance doorways are now not in use for the public. It is good, however, to see the building so largely unspoilt. *Peter Treloar collection/Richard Casserley/MJS*

One of the reasons that thousands of holidaymakers have come to Minehead over the years is Butlin's Holiday Camp, situated less than a mile away along the coast. In a publicity drive in the early 1960s Billy Butlin installed ex-British Railways steam locomotives at some of his camps. This act helped to secure some notable engines for posterity, most of which would no doubt have succumbed to the cutter's torch in scrapyards, but have now found new homes in railway preservation. Withdrawn from 75A Brighton shed in September 1963, ex-SR 'Terrier' 0-6-0T No 32678, one of the two locomotives brought to Minehead, stands in the goods yard at the terminus in the summer of 1977, having come to the railway after Butlin's decided to rid themselves of these static displays. The locomotive subsequently moved on to the Kent & East Sussex Railway in 1983.

In not unusual wet holiday weather, No 32678 is seen at Butlin's on 15 September 1964 in company with the ex-LMS 'Coronation' 4-6-2 No 46229 *Duchess of Hamilton*, the latter having arrived at the camp the previous April. Released from its inglorious incarceration in 1975, having been prey to all weathers, the latter engine, once proud top-link motive power on the West Coast Main Line from Euston to Glasgow, has, in working restoration as part of the National Collection, given immense pleasure to many more thousands than saw it at Minehead, hauling express trains again over BR metals. *Norman Browne/R. E. Toop*

One vital part of any preserved railway is the restoration of rescued motive power, be it steam locomotives, diesels, or coaching and other rolling-stock. On a dull, wet day in 1977 ex-Somerset & Dorset Railway No 88 (withdrawn from 82F Bath (Green Park) shed as BR 53808 in April 1964) stands in the station siding at Minehead, partly sheeted for protection until the time when earnest efforts can be repaid. Built by the Darlington Works of Robert Stephenson & Co in 1925 specifically for the S&DJR, it arrived at Barry Scrapyard in June 1964, from where it was rescued in 1970 by the S&DR Trust. Initially moving to Radstock for restoration, the collapse of this base brought the engine to the WSR, arriving on 9 January 1976. After a prolonged and disjointed rebuild, it finally returned to steam in August 1987.

A little over a decade later, the appearance of the engine belies the fact that it has ever been out of service. Testament to the efforts of the restorers, the powerful locomotive receives attention in the goods yard at Minehead on 10 April 1988, just eight months after its return to steam, somewhat dubiously adorned with an express freight train headcode. At the time of writing it is again in the works, but has so far clocked up just short of 50,000 miles on the WSR. To the right stands No 6412, the railway's stalwart servant from the early days of preservation. *Norman Browne/Tom Heavyside*

Former GWR 4-6-0 No 7820 *Dinmore Manor* is a more modern restoration, being returned to working order in September 1995 with the aid of Birmingham Railway Museum at Tyseley. Built after nationalisation, in November 1950, it was taken out of service exactly 15 years later, in November 1965, from 89A Shrewsbury shed, a victim of the campaign to rid the Western Region of BR of steam traction. After standing in the open in Dai Woodham's yard at Barry Docks, it was moved to the Gwili Railway on 23 September 1979, moving on to the WSR in March 1985. It has taken many years for the locomotive to be restored to working order, but all who have seen it agree that the wait has been worth it and the railway now benefits from this useful, all-purpose addition to its motive power. It is seen here in Minehead goods yard on 13 July 1996. *MJS*

For a final view of the WSR, I make no apologies for returning to pannier tank No 6412. All heritage lines need workhorses and many railways have survived against all odds with, in the early days, just one or two operational locomotives. No 6412 can lay claim to have helped the WSR survive its early years and, as has been seen, with the publicity from the 'Flockton Flyer' it helped also to spread the word. Having been built in November 1934, it was withdrawn from 85B Gloucester (Horton Road) in November 1964, having amassed over 609,000 miles. It then saw preserved service on the Dart Valley Railway from 1966, coming to the WSR ten years later, when its former home considered it surplus to requirements. In March 1978 it is seen here happily without the 'Flyer' adornments, as driver Harry Lee and fireman Frank Houlding prepare themselves and their train for a run to **Williton.** *Peter Triggs*

MINEHEAD BRANCH.

NARROW GAUGE.

Single Line worked by Train Staff. The Staff Stations are Norton Fitzwarren, Williton, Watchet, and Minehead.

Section.	Form of Staff and Tickets.	Colour of Ticket.
Norton Fitzwarren and Williton	.. Square	Red.
Williton and Watchet	.. Triangular	White.
Watchet and Minehead	.. Round	Blue.

Down Trains.   **TAUNTON TO MINEHEAD.**   **Week Days only.**

Miles from Taunton	STATIONS.	1 Goods arr.	dep.	2 Passenger arr.	dep.	3 Goods arr.	dep.	4 Passenger arr.	dep.	5 Passenger arr.	dep.	6 Passenger arr.	dep.	7 Passenger arr.	dep.	8	9
		A.M.	A.M.	A.M.	A.M.	A.M.	A.M.	A.M.	A.M.	P.M.	P.M.	P.M.	P.M.	P.M.	P.M.		
	Taunton 137		6 20		8 0		10 5		11 30		1 55		**A** 4 10		7 0		
2	Norton Fitzwarren	6 26	6 40	8 4	8 5	10 11X	10 25	11 34	11 35	1 59	2 0	4 11	4 15	7 4	X7 5		
2½	Norton Siding							**CR**									
5	Bishop's Lydeard	6 55	7 5	8 14	8 15	10 40	10 48	11 44	11 45	2 7	2 8	4 24	4 25	7 14	7 15		
9	Crowcombe	7 25	7 35	8 26	8 27	11 3	11 10	11 56	11 58	2 18	2 19	4 35	4 36	7 26	7 28		
11¾	Stogumber	7 45	7 55	8 33	8 34	11 19	11 27	12 3	12 5	2 24	2 25	4 41	4 42	7 33	7 35		
15	Williton	8 6	8 15	8 41	X8 43	11 38	X12 25	12 13	X12 16	2 31	X2 33	4 49	X4 51	7 42	X7 44		
16¾	Watchet	X8 20		8 48	X8 49	12 32	12 39	12 19	12 20	2 38	2 39	4 55	4 56	7 48	7 49		
19	Washford			8 55	8 56	12 47	12 52	12 26	12 27	2 45	2 46	5 2	5 3	7 55	7 56		
21¼	Blue Anchor			9 3	9 3			12 32	12 33	2 51	2 52	5 9	5 10	8 2			
23	Dunster			9 8	9 10	1 6	1 13	12 38	12 40	2 58	3 0	5 14	5 16	8 6	8 8		
24¾	**Minehead**			9 15		1 20		12 45		3 5		5 20		8 13			

A Runs on Saturdays only.

CROSSING ARRANGEMENTS BETWEEN NORTON FITZWARREN AND MINEHEAD.

The 6.20 a.m. Train from Taunton will cross the 8.10 a.m. Train from Minehead at Watchet.
The 8.0 a.m. Train from Taunton will cross the 8.10 a.m. Train from Minehead at Williton, and the 8.55 a.m. Train from Watchet at Watchet.
The 10.5 a.m. Train from Taunton will cross the 8.55 a.m. Train from Watchet at Norton Fitzwarren ; the 11.45 a.m. Train from Minehead at Williton, and shunt for the 11.30 a.m. Train from Taunton, at Williton.
The 11.30 a.m. Train from Taunton will cross the 11.45 a.m. from Minehead, and pass the 10.5 a.m. Train from Taunton at Williton.
The 1.55 p.m. Train from Taunton will cross the 2.0 p.m. Train from Minehead at Williton.
The 4.10 p.m. Train from Taunton on Saturdays will cross the 3.40 p.m. Train from Minehead at Williton.
The 7.0 p.m. Train from Taunton will cross the 5.50 p.m. Train from Minehead at Norton Fitzwarren, and on Saturdays it will cross the 7.10 p.m. Train from Minehead at Williton.

Tables 82-83

Above **GWR working timetable, 1886**

Left **BR, Summer 1948**

Right **BR, Winter 1961/2**

94

Table 82 TAUNTON, WATCHET and MINEHEAD

Miles		Week Days am	Week Days am	Week Days am	Week Days am	Week Days pm	Week Days pm	Week Days pm	Week Days pm	Sundays pm H	Sundays am H	Sundays pm H
	61 London (Pad.) 62 .. dep	..	5K30	8 30	1030	1230	..	2 30	6 30	..	11K15	3 30
—	**Taunton** .... dep	7 24	9 50	1125	pm 1 0	3 12	4 25	5 55	9 17	1 15	pm 3 45	6 45
2	Norton Fitzwarren	7 30	..	1129	..	3 16	4 29	5 59	9 21	..	..	..
5	Bishop's Lydeard	7 39	10 0	1136	1 10	3 23	4 36	6 6	9 28	1 25	3 55	6 55
9	Crowcombe	7 47	10 8	1144	1 18	3 31	4 44	6 14	9 35	1 33	4 3	7 3
11¾	Stogumber	7 53	1014	1150	1 24	3 37	4 50	6 21	9 43	1 38	4 8	7 8
15	Williton	8 3	1022	1159	1 33	3 46	5 2	6 29	9 51	1 46	4 16	7 16
16¾	Watchet	8 9	1027	12 4	1 38	3 51	5 7	6 35	9 57	1 51	4 21	7 21
19	Washford	8 17	1034	1211	1 50	3 58	5 15	6 42	10 4	1 58	4 28	7 28
21¼	Blue Anchor	8 22	1039	1216	1 55	4 3	5 20	6 47	10 9	2 3	4 33	7 33
23	Dunster	8 27	1044	1221	2 0	4 8	5 25	6 52	1014	2 8	4 38	7 38
24¾	**Minehead** .... arr	8 32	1049	1226	2 5	4 13	5 30	6 57	1020	2 13	4 43	7 43

Miles		Week Days am	Week Days am	Week Days am	Week Days pm	Week Days pm	Week Days pm	Week Days pm	Week Days pm	Sundays pm H	Sundays pm H	Sundays pm H
—	**Minehead** . .. .. dep	7 35	9 5	1130	1 23	3 15	4 35	6 0	7 30	2 30	5 15	8 5
1¾	Dunster	7 39	9 9	1134	1 27	3 20	4 39	6 4	7 34	2 34	5 19	8 9
3½	Blue Anchor	7 44	9 14	1139	1 32	3 25	4 44	6 9	7 39	2 39	5 24	8 14
5¾	Washford	7 50	9 20	1145	1 38	3 31	4 50	6 15	7 45	2 45	5 30	8 20
8	Watchet	7 56	9 26	1151	1 44	3 38	4 56	6 21	7 51	2 51	5 36	8 26
9¾	Williton	8 3	9 32	12 0	1 51	3 47	5 3	6 27	7 58	2 57	5 42	8 32
13	Stogumber	8 10	9 40	12 7	1 58	3 54	5 10	6 37	8 5	3 4	5 49	8 39
15¾	Crowcombe	8 17	9 47	1214	2 5	4 1	5 17	6 44	8 12	3 11	5 56	8 46
19¾	Bishop's Lydeard	8 24	9 54	1222	2 12	4 9	5 25	6 52	8 20	3 18	6 3	8 53
22¾	Norton Fitzwarren	8 30	10 0	1228	....	4 15	5 31	6 58	8 26	....	....	....
24¾	**Taunton** .. .. .. arr	8 35	10 5	1233	2 22	4 20	5 38	7 3	8 31	3 28	6 13	9 3
167¾	61 London (Pad.) 62 .. arr	1115	pm 1 20	3 25	4 55	7 20	9 13	....	....	7 20	9 25	am 3K25

H Runs 17th and 24th September, 1961 and commencing 20th May, 1962

K Via Bristol

A limited Road Motor Service is operated by the Western National Omnibus Company between Minehead, Porlock Village and Lynmouth

For OTHER TRAINS between Taunton and Norton Fitzwarren, see Tables 81 and 86

Table 83 TAUNTON, CHARD CENTRAL and CHARD JUNCTION

WEEK DAYS ONLY

Miles		am	am	am	am	pm	pm S	pm	pm	pm	pm	pm	pm	pm
—	**Taunton** .. .. .. dep	6 0	..	8 0	..	..	..	3 12	..	4 30	..	..	6 45	..
3½	Thornfalcon	..	..	8 6	..	..	..	3 20	..	4 36	..	..	6 52	..
6½	Hatch	..	..	8 14	..	..	..	3 29	..	4 44	..	..	7 0	..
9¾	Ilton Halt	..	..	8 22	..	..	..	3 37	..	4 52	..	..	7 8	..
11¼	Ilminster	6 40	..	8 28	..	..	..	3 43	..	4 58	..	..	7 13	..
12	Donyatt Halt	..	..	8 32	..	..	..	3 49	..	5 2	..	..	7 17	..
15¼	**Chard Central** .. arr	7 0	..	8 40	..	..	..	3 57	..	5 10	..	..	7 25	..
	dep	..	8 10	..	9 34	12 2	1 52	..	4 7	..	5 30	6 9	..	8 43
18½	**Chard Junction** .... arr	..	8 18	..	9 42	1210	2 0	..	4 15	..	5 38	6 17	..	8 51

Miles		am	am	am	pm	pm	pm S	pm	pm	pm	pm	pm
—	**Chard Junction** .. dep	8 28	..	1056	1245	..	2 30	5 4	5 50	6 34	..	9 30
3¼	**Chard Central** .. arr	8 37	..	11 6	1255	..	2 39	5 13	5 59	6 43	..	9 39
	dep	..	8 45	..	..	1 35	..	5 15	..	..	7 40	9 45
6½	Donyatt Halt	..	8 51	..	..	1 41	..	5 21	..	..	7 46	..
7¼	Ilminster	..	8 55	..	..	1 47	..	5 25	..	..	7 51	9 53
8¾	Ilton Halt	..	8 58	..	..	1 51	..	5 29	..	..	7 55	..
12	Hatch	..	9 5	..	..	2 0	..	5 36	..	..	8 2	..
15	Thornfalcon	..	9 12	..	..	2 7	..	5 43	..	..	8 9	..
18½	**Taunton** .. .. .. arr	..	9 21	..	..	2 15	..	5 56	..	..	8 17	1016

S Saturdays only

A: OFF-PEAK SERVICE

	1	2 [D]	3	4 [D]
MINEHEAD dep.	10.15	12.15	2.25	4.00
Dunster	10.21	12.21	2.31	4.06
Blue Anchor	10.29	12.27	2.39	4.12
Washford	10.38	12.35	2.48	4.20
Watchet	10.46	12.43	2.56	4.28
Doniford Beach (R)	10.50	12.45	3.00	4.32
Williton	10.58	12.54	3.04	4.40
Stogumber	11.09	1.03	3.15	4.49
Crowcombe Heathfield	11.19	1.10	3.25	4.56
BISHOPS LYDEARD arr.	11.29	1.20	3.35	5.06

	1	2	3	4
BISHOPS LYDEARD dep.	10.25	12.20	2.35	4.05
Crowcombe Heathfield	10.35	12.34	2.45	4.19
Stogumber	10.42	12.42	2.52	4.27
Williton	10.56	12.52	3.06	4.37
Doniford Beach (R)	10.59	12.55	3.09	4.40
Watchet	11.03	12.58	3.13	4.43
Washford	11.11	1.07	3.21	4.52
Blue Anchor	11.18	1.14	3.28	4.59
Dunster	11.24	1.21	3.34	5.06
MINEHEAD arr.	11.30	1.27	3.40	5.13

TAUNTON BUS LINK SERVICE – Saturdays only

Taunton Castleway	11.15	3.25
Taunton BR Station	11.20	3.30
Bishops Lydeard Station	11.35	3.50
Bishops Lydeard Station	11.45	3.55
Taunton BR Station	12.00	4.15
Taunton Castleway	12.05	4.20

B: LOW PEAK SERVICE

	1	2	3	4 [X]
MINEHEAD dep.	10.15	12.10	2.25	4.40
Dunster	10.21	12.16	2.31	4.46
Blue Anchor	10.29	12.24	2.39	5.02
Washford	10.38	12.33	2.48	5.11
Watchet	10.46	12.41	2.56	5.19
Doniford Beach (R)	10.50	12.45	3.00	5.23
Williton	10.58	12.53	3.04	5.27
Stogumber	11.09	1.04	3.15	5.38
Crowcombe Heathfield	11.19	1.14	3.25	5.48
BISHOPS LYDEARD arr.	11.29	1.24	3.35	5.58

	1	2	3 [X]	4
BISHOPS LYDEARD dep.	10.25	12.20	2.30	4.05
Crowcombe Heathfield	10.39	12.34	2.44	4.19
Stogumber	10.47	12.42	2.52	4.27
Williton	10.57	12.52	3.06	4.37
Doniford Beach (R)	11.00	12.55	3.09	4.40
Watchet	11.03	12.58	3.12	4.43
Washford	11.12	1.07	3.21	4.52
Blue Anchor	11.19	1.14	3.28	4.59
Dunster	11.26	1.21	3.35	5.06
MINEHEAD arr.	11.32	1.27	3.41	5.13

X – On the dates marked with a box in the calendar, these services will be DIESEL-hauled. [D]

TAUNTON BUS LINK SERVICE – Saturdays only

Taunton Castleway	11.15	3.25
Taunton BR Station	11.20	3.30
Bishops Lydeard Station	11.35	3.50
Bishops Lydeard Station	11.45	3.55
Taunton BR Station	12.00	4.15
Taunton Castleway	12.05	4.20

C: PEAK SERVICE

	1	2	3	4	5 [D]	6	7 [D]	8
MINEHEAD dep.	10.15	11.10	12.10	2.00	2.55	3.50	4.45	5.35
Dunster	10.21	11.16	12.16	2.06	3.01	3.56	4.51	5.41
Blue Anchor	10.30	11.28	12.25	2.15	3.14	4.05	5.05	5.49
Washford	10.39	11.36	12.34	2.24	3.22	4.14	5.13	5.59
Watchet	10.49	11.43	12.44	2.34	3.29	4.24	5.20	6.06
Doniford Beach (R)	10.53	11.46	12.48	2.38	3.32	4.28	5.23	6.10
Williton	11.01	11.49	12.56	2.48	3.35	4.39	5.27	6.18
Stogumber	11.13	—	1.08	3.00	—	4.51	—	6.29
Crowcombe Heathfield	11.23		1.18	3.10		4.59		6.39
BISHOPS LYDEARD arr.	11.33		1.28	3.20		5.09		6.49

	1	2	3	4 [D]	5	6	7 [D]	8
BISHOPS LYDEARD dep.		10.25		12.20	2.10		4.05	5.45
Crowcombe Heathfield		10.39		12.35	2.24		4.19	5.59
Stogumber	—	10.48	—	12.43	2.33	—	4.28	6.07
Williton	10.00	11.00	11.58	12.55	2.48	3.40	4.38	6.17
Doniford Beach (R)	10.03	11.05	12.01	1.00	2.52	3.43	4.43	6.20
Watchet	10.07	11.09	12.05	1.04	2.57	3.47	4.47	6.23
Washford	10.15	11.17	12.13	1.12	3.05	3.55	4.55	6.31
Blue Anchor	10.32	11.25	12.28	1.20	3.13	4.07	5.03	6.38
Dunster	10.38	11.32	12.34	1.27	3.19	4.13	5.10	6.45
MINEHEAD arr.	10.44	11.39	12.40	1.34	3.27	4.19	5.17	6.51

TAUNTON BUS LINK SERVICE

	WSO		SO	SO	
Taunton Castleway	09.45	11.45	1.10	3.05	4.45
Taunton BR Station	09.50	11.50	1.20	3.15	4.50
Bishops Lydeard Station	10.10	12.05	1.40	3.35	5.10

	SO		SO		WSO
Bishops Lydeard Station	12.10	1.45	3.45	5.15	7.00
Taunton BR Station	12.25	2.05	4.05	5.30	7.15
Taunton Castleway	12.30	2.15	4.15	5.35	7.20

WSO – Wednesdays & Saturdays only   SO – Saturdays only

D: HIGH PEAK SERVICE

	1	2 [D]	3	4	5	6	7 [D]	8
MINEHEAD dep.	10.15	11.10	12.10	2.00	2.55	3.50	4.45	5.35
Dunster	10.21	11.16	12.16	2.06	3.01	3.56	4.51	5.41
Blue Anchor	10.30	11.30	12.25	2.15	3.16	4.05	5.06	5.49
Washford	10.39	11.39	12.34	2.24	3.25	4.14	5.15	5.59
Watchet	10.49	11.46	12.44	2.34	3.35	4.24	5.24	6.06
Doniford Beach (R)	10.53	11.49	12.48	2.38	3.39	4.28	5.28	6.10
Williton	11.01	12.00	12.56	2.48	3.45	4.39	5.33	6.18
Stogumber	11.13	12.11	1.08	3.00	3.58	4.51	5.46	6.29
Crowcombe Heathfield	11.27	12.37	1.18	3.10	4.21	4.59	6.02	6.39
BISHOPS LYDEARD arr.	11.37	12.47	1.28	3.20	4.31	5.09	6.12	6.49

	1 [D]	2	3	4	5	6	7	8
BISHOPS LYDEARD dep.	09.30	10.25	11.10	12.20	1.05	2.10	4.05	5.45
Crowcombe Heathfield	09.40	10.39	11.25	12.35	1.25	2.24	4.19	5.59
Stogumber	09.49	10.48	11.34	12.43	1.34	2.33	4.28	6.07
Williton	10.00	11.00	11.55	12.55	1.47	2.48	4.38	6.17
Doniford Beach (R)	10.04	11.05	11.59	1.00	1.50	2.52	4.43	6.20
Watchet	10.08	11.09	12.05	1.04	1.54	2.57	4.47	6.23
Washford	10.17	11.17	12.14	1.12	2.03	3.05	4.55	6.31
Blue Anchor	10.32	11.25	12.28	1.20	2.18	3.13	5.03	6.38
Dunster	10.39	11.32	12.35	1.27	2.24	3.19	5.10	6.45
MINEHEAD arr.	10.45	11.39	12.41	1.34	2.31	3.27	5.17	6.51

TAUNTON BUS LINK SERVICE

Taunton Castleway	11.45	4.45
Taunton BR Station	11.50	4.50
Bishops Lydeard Station	12.05	5.10
Bishops Lydeard Station	12.05	5.15
Taunton BR Station	12.25	5.30
Taunton Castleway	12.30	5.35

WHY NOT JOIN US?

The WSR Association actively supports the Railway. Members receive a range of excellent benefits and new members are always welcome. Details: The Station, Bishops Lydeard, Taunton, TA4 3BX.

WSR, 1997

INDEX OF LOCATIONS